AIR CAMPAIGN

OPERATION *STEINBOCK* 1944
The Luftwaffe's disastrous last Blitz over England

CHRIS GOSS | ILLUSTRATED BY ADAM TOOBY

OSPREY PUBLISHING
Bloomsbury Publishing Plc
Kemp House, Chawley Park, Cumnor Hill, Oxford OX2 9PH, UK
29 Earlsfort Terrace, Dublin 2, Ireland
1385 Broadway, 5th Floor, New York, NY 10018, USA
E-mail: info@ospreypublishing.com
www.ospreypublishing.com

OSPREY is a trademark of Osprey Publishing Ltd

First published in Great Britain in 2025

© Osprey Publishing Ltd, 2025

All rights reserved. No part of this publication may be reproduced or transmitted in any form or by any means, electronic or mechanical, including photocopying, recording, or any information storage or retrieval system, without prior permission in writing from the publishers.

A catalogue record for this book is available from the British Library.

ISBN: PB 9781472855329; eBook 9781472855305; ePDF 9781472855299; XML 9781472855312

25 26 27 28 29 10 9 8 7 6 5 4 3 2 1

Maps by www.bounford.com
Diagrams by Adam Tooby
3D BEVs by Paul Kime
Index by Fionbar Lyons
Typeset by PDQ Digital Media Solutions, Bungay, UK
Printed by Repro India Ltd.
Title page: See caption on p. 91.

Osprey Publishing supports the Woodland Trust, the UK's leading woodland conservation charity.

To find out more about our authors and books visit www.ospreypublishing.com. Here you will find extracts, author interviews, details of forthcoming events and the option to sign up for our newsletter.

Acknowledgements
I would like to thank (in no particular order) the following who helped with this book:
Bernd Rauchbach (Germany), Sebastian Remus (Germany), Brian Bines (UK), Andy Saunders (UK), Rene Millet (Germany), Ian White (UK), Ian Thirsk (UK), Nick Beale (UK), Robert Forsyth (UK), Sven Carlson (Germany), Jeremy Green (USA), Simon Trew (UK) and Andy Thomas (UK).
If I have forgotten anyone, it is not deliberate and I apologise.
Chris Goss
Marlow, 2024
All photos are from the Author's Collection except where stated.

AIR CAMPAIGN

CONTENTS

INTRODUCTION	4
CHRONOLOGY	7
ATTACKER'S CAPABILITIES	8
DEFENDER'S CAPABILITIES	18
CAMPAIGN OBJECTIVES	26
THE CAMPAIGN	31
ANALYSIS AND CONCLUSION	86
BIBLIOGRAPHY	94
INDEX	95

INTRODUCTION

Reichsmarschall Hermann Göring – a highly decorated World War I fighter pilot whose achievements in the next war left much to be desired. (Author's collection)

On 7 December 1943, Dr Joseph Goebbels, the Reich Minister for Propaganda, wrote:

> Göring has now gone west to prepare the reprisal attacks against England. For this we need about 200 heavy four-engined aircraft which will in one night fly to England twice and deliver a massive blow against the capital. Of course, we cannot carry out an attack like this often enough but it should serve as a reminder to the English that we are still around.

This statement arose from a conference held on 28 November 1943 in which Reichsmarschall Hermann Göring had stated the following to Luftwaffe senior officers:

> Gentlemen, the matter I am now going to discuss with you is one of the strictest secrecy; the matter of the preparation and execution of reprisals against England, the first attack to be on London. First of all there are the units which General Peltz, Angriffsführer England, already has as the commander responsible for this operation. These units must now be replenished with aircraft more rapidly. The Director of Air Armaments is to do everything possible in a special effort in the next few days…
>
> I have told the Führer we shall be ready in 14 days. It is absolutely necessary that we have 300 aircraft ready for the first operation. If I can have some 100 in the second raid and early in the morning about 150, then that is 550–600 sorties; that is our objective!

The 29-year-old General Dietrich Peltz, a former Stuka and highly experienced Ju 88 pilot who had already been awarded the Knight's Cross of the Iron Cross with Oak Leaves and Swords in July 1943 (the 31st member of the German armed forces to receive such an award), had been given the task of General der Kampfflieger in January 1943 and Angriffsführer England in March 1943 with the aim of coordinating and intensifying bombing attacks on mainland Britain. In August 1943, he took command of IX Fliegerkorps which was based at Le Coudray-en-Theile, south of Beauvais in northern France, and with it nine different Geschwader equipped with five different types of bomber. IX Fliegerkorps was subordinate to Luftflotte 3 in Paris commanded by Generalfeldmarschall Hugo Sperrle.

After the war, Peltz made known his concerns for this offensive. To cause and sustain fires at targets required more aircraft than he had at his disposal. He could not attack on moonlit nights because he knew that there would be serious losses at the hands of the superlative RAF nightfighters. Paradoxically, with moonless nights, the poor training most of his crews had received meant that they were unlikely to find let alone accurately bomb their targets. However, he was forced to accept his task, later saying:

> It was a question of duty. If the Allies were destroying German cities day after day, the German people expected the Luftwaffe to retaliate against British cities and we in the German bomber force had to do the best we could with the forces we had. What alternative was there?

On 3 December 1943, Göring wrote to his senior commanders laying out what was expected and that it would commence at the end of the full-moon period that month. What he expected was overly optimistic and it would take the Luftwaffe another month to be in any position to start any meaningful offensive.

However, things were not as easy as Göring had anticipated. Despite Luftflotte 3 announcing that *Steinbock* – as the offensive was now codenamed, this appearing first in documents dated 19 December 1943 – would begin on 31 December 1943, the operational units were by no means ready as all units were way below strength in respect of the numbers of combat-ready aircraft and crews. For example, on 25 December 1943, of Kampfgeschwader 6's (KG 6's) strength of 33 Junkers Ju 188s, only 15 were combat-ready; while of its 41 crews, only 28 were combat-ready. Stab and I./KG 51 were in the process of converting from the Ju 88 to the Messerschmitt Me 410,

Generalmajor Dietrich Peltz, General der Kampfflieger – a successful Stuka and bomber pilot who in just three years was promoted from Hauptmann to be the youngest general in the German armed services. He played a major part in *Steinbock*. (Author's collection)

Peltz inspecting the Do 217 unit III./KG 2. He became General der Kampfflieger in January 1943. (Author's collection)

and despite having a strength of 40 aircraft, only 16 were combat-ready; and of its 38 crews, only one was combat-ready. Finally, the pathfinders of I./KG 66, which would be crucial to any offensive, were in the process of being modified so of its 33 Ju 88S and Ju 188s, only three were available. Furthermore, in respect of reserve aircraft, there were only four Ju 188s, one Ju 88S, 20 Ju 88s, three Me 410s and six Focke-Wulf Fw 190s available. It was clear that the start of *Steinbock* would now have to slip into January 1944.

The first attacks of 1944 came on the night of 2 January 1944, which was a minor attack on London carried out by Fw 190s of I./Schnellkampfgeschwader 10 (I./SKG 10) and Me 410s of V./KG 2. A further four attacks then occurred up to 20 January 1944, the five attacks costing the Luftwaffe five Fw 190s, four Me 410s and crucially two Ju 88S pathfinders from I./KG 66. Unusually, during this period, the RAF did not intercept any German radio traffic which would have indicated that an offensive was being planned but did note that German air activity was unusually slight.

The last two German combat losses before the commencement of Operation *Steinbock* occurred on the night of 15 January 1943 when Feldwebel (Fw) Georg Sprint and Oberfeldwebel (Ofw) Rudolf Berghäuser of 2./SKG 10 failed to return from an attack on London, one of them being shot down by Sqn Ldr Alastair Parker-Rees and his Navigator/Radar Operator (Nav/Rad) Flt Lt Geoff Bennett of 96 Sqn 10–15 miles south of Dungeness at 2009hrs. For the next six days, things were very quiet in the night skies over Britain as there must have been frantic activity at German airfields to get aircraft and crews ready. Then, for the night of 21 January 1944, British intelligence reported:

> After a long period of scattered or relatively small attacks, enemy air activity flared up on Friday/Saturday night when London was the primary target and 92 aircraft were plotted overland, the largest force to attack land targets on any one night since 29/30 July 1942 when 100 long-range bombers made penetrations and Birmingham was the main target. *Steinbock* or the Baby Blitz had at last begun.

Operational units of IX Fliegerkorps as of 25 December 1943					
Unit	Aircraft	Strength	Available	Crews	Crews ready
KG 2	Do 217	65	57	81	63
	Ju 188	28	20	40	23
	Me 410	21	11	25	14
KG 6	Ju 188	33	15	41	28
	Ju 88	63	45	80	60
KG 30	Ju 88	60	54	74	58
KG 54	Ju 88	50	44	85	72
I./KG 76	Ju 88	31	20	37	20
Stab, I./KG 51	Me 410	40	24	36	1
I./SKG 10	Fw 190	22	16	38	21
I./KG 100	He 177	15	7	11	11*
KG 66	Ju 88S/188	33	3	34	15**
Reserves	Ju 188	4			
	Ju 88S	1			
	Ju 88	20			
	Me 410	3			
	Fw 190	6			
* Additional four aircraft at Châteaudun, three at Lechfeld and nine with KG 40; four crews at Lechfeld and eight crews with KG 40					
** Aircraft being modified					

CHRONOLOGY

1940
18 June First major nocturnal attack by Luftwaffe against mainland UK targets.

22 June Battle of France ends with French surrender.

10 July Battle of Britain officially begins with attacks against coastal targets.

12 August Attacks now include radar stations and airfields.

7 September Target switches from airfields to London as well as other cities and industrial targets.

30 September Last major daylight attack on London.

29 October Last major daylight attack of the Battle of Britain.

1941
16 April Luftwaffe attacks Yugoslavia and Greece, having moved a number of bomber Geschwader in preparation.

10 May Last night of the main Blitz against London, after which many more German bomber Geschwader move to the Eastern Front in preparation for Operation *Barbarossa*, which begins 22 June.

1942
24 April Baedeker Blitz begins.

30 July Heaviest attack since May 1941 against Birmingham by 76 aircraft.

19 August Dieppe invasion sees heavy losses to Dornier Do 217 units KG 2 and II./KG 40.

31 October Last Baedeker-related attack against Canterbury.

1943
28 November Generalfeldmarschall Göring announces intention to carry out major attacks against London and other cities in reprisal for attacks on German cities.

3 December Outline for *Steinbock* released.

31 December Start date postponed.

1944
21 January First *Steinbock* attacks against London.

22 January Allied landings at Nettuno and Anzio divert Luftwaffe assets.

19 April Last attack on London by just 18 aircraft.

20 April Hull attacked.

24 April First attack on Bristol.

25 April First attack on Portsmouth.

29 April Attack on Plymouth which also saw use of Fritz X guided bombs.

28 May Attack on Torquay.

29 May Attack on Falmouth.

6 June Allies land in Normandy.

Generalfeldmarschall Hugo Sperrle was in command of Luftflotte 3 from before the war until replaced in August 1944 – another Great War veteran who did not do as well as Hermann Göring. (Author's collection)

ATTACKER'S CAPABILITIES
The Luftwaffe in the West in 1944

Me 410A-1 seen here from 13./KG 2. The successor of the inadequate Me 210, it was operated by V./KG 2 (later II./KG 51) in the intruder, nuisance, bomber and pathfinding roles from July 1943. I./KG 51 would also take part in the latter part of *Steinbock* in the pure bombing role. (Author's collection)

Context

The Luftwaffe bomber force which now faced Britain was a shadow of what faced Britain in the Battle of Britain and the Blitz. Forced to fight on the Eastern Front from June 1941, the Mediterranean and North Africa from April 1941 and with America joining the war in December 1941, it was no surprise that Germany was now on the retreat, especially having been forced out of North Africa and into Italy. As to the reasons for *Steinbock*, there appears to be no other reason than to bomb the British capital in revenge and as a boost to German morale, especially in those towns and cities being bombed by the USAAF in daylight and the RAF by night, whatever the cost to the German bomber units. However, it was General Dietrich Peltz who best summed up the task ahead:

> The political directive I received which came from Hitler via Göring was to attack London. Personally I should have preferred not to have bombed the cities. I would have preferred to attack British power stations. These were small pin-point targets that would have been difficult to hit but I think that we could have done so by using our best crews at low-level at night. Of course there would be losses. From our experience of Allied attacks on German cities, I knew that the time needed to recover from the effects of a bombing attack was remarkably short but if we could pick off the power stations, I think we should have had more effect in the long run.

Despite Peltz's reservations, Hermann Göring made it clear on 3 December 1943 by writing:

> To avenge the terror attacks of the enemy I have decided to intensify the air war over the British Isles by means of concentrated attacks on cities and especially industrial centres and ports.

As it was – an He 111 approaching London over Essex in September 1940. Following the Luftwaffe's failure in the Battle of Britain, no further massed daylight attacks took place by German bombers, which now used darkness as a means to help survivability. (Author's collection)

Aircraft

By the end of 1943, two bomber types were no longer able to survive in the skies over Britain. Due to heavy losses in the Battle of France and Battle of Britain, production of the Do 17 finished in October 1940 and crews then either converted to the Ju 88 or the Do 17's direct replacement the Do 217 (from mid-1941). The Heinkel He 111 was also starting to be replaced by the summer of 1940 with crews also converting to the Ju 88. The He 111's restricted range and bombload (the He 111H-6 had a range of just under 1,500 miles and a bombload of just under 4,500lbs) prevented it from being a truly long-range bomber capable of reaching targets well inside the Soviet Union but it could still theoretically be used over Great Britain. However, during the Battle of Britain, it was proven to be vulnerable to fighter attack and by the end of 1943, the RAF's nightfighter aircraft were much improved, heavily armed and fitted with Airborne Interception (AI) radar. Back in 1940, the He 111's defensive armament had to be increased to cope with the fighter threat, which at the same time forced increasing its normal crew of a pilot, *Beobachter* (observer), *Bordfunker* (radio operator) and *Bordmechaniker* (flight engineer – the latter three also acting as gunners) by an additional gunner; even this would not be enough and as a result, the He 111 was kept well away from the front line in the west even at night. It was hoped that the He 111 could be replaced by the four-engined He 177, but despite this type first flying in November 1939, it was plagued by development and mechanical problems and political interference, and even though the He 177 at last flew its first missions against shipping in the Atlantic and the Mediterranean in November 1943 (suffering heavy losses in the second attack), it had to wait for the first night of *Steinbock* to be used in conventional bombing attacks and even then in minimal numbers.

Peltz therefore had six types of aircraft available to him for the start of *Steinbock* in the bomber, pathfinder, intruder and fighter-bomber roles. The Do 217 was already becoming obsolete and equipped just two Gruppen from KG 2. The Ju 88 equipped six Gruppen while the Ju 88S formed a mixed Ju 88/188 pathfinding Gruppe. The Ju 188 equipped two Gruppen while the He 177 equipped just three Staffel from two different Geschwader (I./KG 40 and I./KG 100). Finally, the Fw 190 and Me 410 equipped one Gruppe each; the latter would be joined by an additional Gruppe in February 1944. This totalled a maximum strength of 524 bombers as of 20 January 1944.

The Do 17 quickly proved itself vulnerable to RAF fighters during the Battle of Britain – this one from 2./KG 76 was lucky to get back on 15 September 1940. It was approaching obsolescence even by the start of war and most units had converted to other types with production of this type ceasing in October 1940. (Author's collection)

The Do 217 came in two versions – the radial-engined K and the in-line liquid-cooled M. Both had a top speed of around 340mph and a service ceiling of 29,500ft (K) and 24,150ft (M). Both had a range when fully laden of around 1,300 miles and a bombload of around 8,800lbs.

The Ju 88, the so-called '*Schnellbomber*', came in a number of variants, the most up to date being the Ju 88A-14, which essentially was an improved Ju 88A-4 with a range of 1,560 miles, maximum altitude of 26,500ft and a maximum speed of 265mph. Its maximum bombload was 6,600lbs. The Ju 88S was an aerodynamically refined version of the A-4 with removal of the gondola, dive brakes and external racks giving it a top speed of 375mph at 26,000ft. Its maximum bombload was reduced to 4,400lbs and its crew reduced to three. This aircraft was only used by I./KG 66 as a pathfinder.

The Ju 188 came as A and E variants with a range of 1,500 miles, maximum altitude of 33,000ft and a top speed of around 320mph. It could also carry 6,600lbs of bombs.

Similar could be said of the He 111 in the Battle of Britain – this one from Stab II./KG 53 managed to get back on 5 September 1940 only for the same crew to be shot down and captured on 15 September 1940. A common sight during the early years of the war and other theatres of operations, it had been replaced in the west by other types by the time of *Steinbock*. (Author's collection)

Do 217 M-1 Wk Nr 56125 U5+UK. This aircraft was damaged in an accident at Eindhoven on 7 September 1943 and once repaired became U5+CT of 9./KG 2, and was reported missing attacking Hull on the night of 20 April 1944; Ogefr Hermann Wendt and his crew were all killed. (Author's collection)

The aircraft yet to be tested as a conventional bomber was the He 177. Plagued with all sorts of technical problems not helped by twin engines powering one airscrew on each wing, it was only available in limited numbers to IX Fliegerkorps but had a top speed of 295mph, maximum altitude of 26,500ft and a range of around 3,100 miles. It had a maximum bombload of 13,200lbs but this was rarely achieved. The shortcoming of this type is best summed up by Peltz:

> It was true that the He 177 carried the greatest bombload of the types under my command but she was technically very complicated. Because of this, the number of aircraft available for any one mission was very low in comparison with the other types.

The smaller types available to Peltz were the Me 410 and Fw 190. The two-seater Me 410 was used both as an intruder, bomber, nightfighter and pathfinder by V./KG 2 (which was redesignated II./KG 51 in March 1944) and a bomber by I./KG 51. It had a maximum speed of 385mph, service ceiling of 32,800ft and a range of 1,400 miles, and could carry up to 2,200lbs of bombs. The Fw 190 was operated by I./SKG 10 in the A-5 and G-3 variants, the G-3 being designed specifically as a long-range fighter-bomber. It had a maximum speed of just under 400mph, service ceiling of just under 35,000ft but a range of just under 600 miles using internal fuel only. It could carry a single 500kg (1,100lb) bomb but more normally carried a single 250kg bomb with the ability to carry four 50kg bombs if external wing tanks were not carried.

Navigation

The Germans had, from the start of the war, a precision VHF radio beam navigation and bombing system known as *Knickebein*. By using a powerful transmitter, an intersection of two narrow beams produced an accurate position fix. Positioning such an intersection over the target and using the standard Lorenz blind approach receiver allowed crews to bomb blindly with a degree of accuracy.

The successor to Knickebein was X-Verfahren and required the installation of X-Gerät equipment on He 111s of Kampfgruppe 100 (KGr 100). It worked on the same principle as Knickebein, using a main approach beam with three cross beams which, with a manual timer, checked the aircraft's speed over the ground and then provided automatic bomb release.

This was followed by Y-Verfahren, which was initially used by He 111s of III./KG 26. This used a single beam to provide track guidance together with a distance-measuring facility. The beam was produced by a transmitter which broadcast three directional signals per second with signals of equal duration with a dividing gap. A second ground station would measure the bomber's distance out along the beam by sending a modulated signal that triggered

Ju 88S-1 of I./KG 66 photographed on 19 March 1944. The Ju 88S was an aerodynamically refined version of the A-4, with the removal of the gondola, dive brakes and external racks giving it a top speed of 375mph, but its maximum bombload was reduced to 4,400lbs and its crew reduced to three. (Author's collection)

a transponder on the He 111 and sent a signal back. This allowed the ground station to measure the distance from the aircraft to the station and therefore the distance to the target. When the aircraft's distance matched that of the target distance, instructions were sent for bombs to be released.

By 1944, the Luftwaffe still used Knickebein and Y-Verfahren but had also developed Freya EGON, EGON standing for Erstling Gemse Offensive Navigation system. Erstling was the codename of the FuG 25a transceiver in the aircraft and Gemse was the codename for the receiver. The system operated on a principle similar to the RAF OBOE navigation system where a signal was sent from Freya radar, which had its receiver antenna removed, to the aircraft. The FuG 25a in the aircraft responded and the received signal was displayed as a range offset on the Freya display. Using a second transmitter and triangulation, the position of the aircraft was pinpointed.

A further navigation aid was employed by I./KG 66, which used captured British GEE sets and named the devices *Hyperbel Gerät* (hyperbola device) but codenamed them *Truhe Gerät* (chest device). It measured the time delay between two radio signals to produce a fix, with accuracy to the order of a few hundred metres at ranges up to about 350 miles. It was the first hyperbolic navigation system to be used operationally, utilising a system where a receiver is used to determine location using the difference in timing of radio waves received from radio navigation beacon transmitters. One of the reasons why many of I./KG 66's aircraft were not ready is believed to be as a result of them being fitted with these newer navigational and blind-bombing systems.

Working on a Ju 188 of KG 2 – note the spinners have been removed. KG 2 had carried out the Luftwaffe's bomber war against Britain from 1940 onwards, its Do 17s being replaced by Do 217s, and by late 1943 this type was starting to be replaced by the Ju 188. (Author's collection)

A Freya radar site seen here at Cherbourg. A signal sent by Freya radar and received by aircraft was displayed as a range offset on the Freya display, and by using a second transmitter and triangulation, the position of the aircraft could be pinpointed. (Author's collection)

Target marking

Pathfinding for *Steinbock* was performed by the Ju 88S and Ju 188s of Maj Hermann Schmidt's I./KG 66, which was based at Montdidier, and Me 410s of II./KG 51. Crews would fly the same course, which would be used by the main bomber force using specialist radio aids such as EGON and Truhe. However, as they crossed the English coast, they generally turned off such equipment so as not to give advance warning of an attack. They then followed four distinct tasks for target marking.

The first task was known as the '*Wendepunkt Markierer*' or turning point marker, the point at which the main force had to turn to take the correct course to the target. Aircraft would drop 18 or 20 LC50 parachute flares with pre-selected colours of red, white, green or yellow which had a duration of illumination of around 20 minutes. If the turning point was over the sea, they would drop See-Lux markers which burned on the sea's surface.

The second task was performed by the *Zielfinder* or target marker, usually by an experienced crew, which preceded the main attack by around ten minutes. When the target was reached, ground markers were dropped. This was known as the *Ablauflinie* (run-up line) – the track for the run-up to the target was set 6km from the edge of the target area at right angles to the planned line of approach. When poor weather conditions prevailed, the run-up was marked by a line of seven white or alternate white and coloured sky markers covering a distance of 6km from the edge of the target area, this line of flares was known as the *Leuchtpfad* (light path).

The third task was the *Zielmarkierer* or target markers, who would follow the Zielfinder and then drop incendiaries onto the target. The final task was then performed by aircraft known as *Beleuchter* or target illuminators who would drop flares as an additional guide. This could be done by any aircraft with a suitably experienced crew.

14 ATTACKER'S CAPABILITIES

OPPOSITE LUFTWAFFE TARGET MARKING METHODS

These illustrations are based on sketches that appeared in an RAF Intelligence report dated 8 February 1944. Information was obtained from prisoners taken from aircraft shot down during the raids against London on 21–22 and 29–30 January. Two of the sketches were based on drawings contained in a notebook found on one of the airmen; a good example of what could happen when rules forbidding the carrying of documents and personal papers during operational sorties were disobeyed.

The drawings show procedures believed to have been adopted by I./KG 66 (and some other units) to mark ground targets, and the final approach to those targets, during the opening stages of *Steinbock*. Sketch 1 illustrates methods to be used in conditions of clear visibility, while sketches 2–4 show what was to be done when there was patchy cloud cover.

Evidence exists that efforts were made to use these techniques during the first London raids. For example, the method shown in sketch 3 was attempted on 21–22 January, while procedures shown in sketches 1 and 4 were tried eight nights later. Captured orders also demonstrated that an '*Ablauflinie*' was supposed to be used in at least one of these raids. However, the British failed to detect a single example of a correctly laid *Ablauflinie* and the poor accuracy achieved during the first four attacks on London hardly speaks volumes for the Luftwaffe's success in implementing orders of this kind.

From 18 February onwards, the Germans abandoned these rather elaborate procedures, ordering their crews to drop their bombs on clusters of coloured flares that would be provided by the pathfinders and renewed throughout the duration of the raid. Generally speaking, this method was more successful – although even then there were conspicuous failures, notably at Bristol and Hull, where gross navigational errors caused flares and bombs alike to be dropped many miles from their intended targets on several different occasions.

Note: The references to white, red and green sky marker flares, and to white and green incendiary bombs, are as they appear in the original document. But the British failed to identify any incendiaries that burned with a green flame, and flares could in fact be coloured differently from those mentioned here (e.g. yellow or orange).

It is interesting to note that the Allies detailed German pathfinding in a document dated 26 December 1943, five days before the expected start of *Steinbock*, stating:

> The German Air Force, always quick to adopt a good idea from the enemy, has recently been experimenting with pathfinder procedures on night operations. So far, no significant success has rewarded their efforts. It appears though that although the German Air Force is making use of a pathfinder procedure more frequently, it is not proving very successful. In spite of the use of Düppel (chaff) to jam Allied radar equipment, the pathfinder aircraft have been located and intercepted. In the attack on Lincoln 17–18 August 1943, the pathfinder technique was used and was a complete failure. The nearest bomb to Lincoln fell 15 miles away. In fact, this raid would never have been recognised if the German radio had not broadcast a description of the target.

Ju 188 of I./KG 66. KG 66 was a pathfinder unit initially flying the Do 217s, then a mix of Ju 188s and Ju 88S-1s. It played an active part in *Steinbock*. (Author's collection)

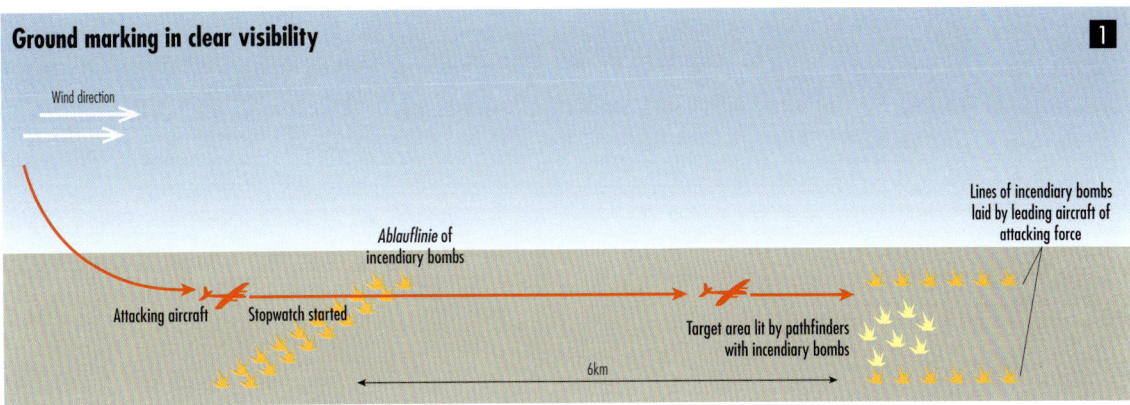
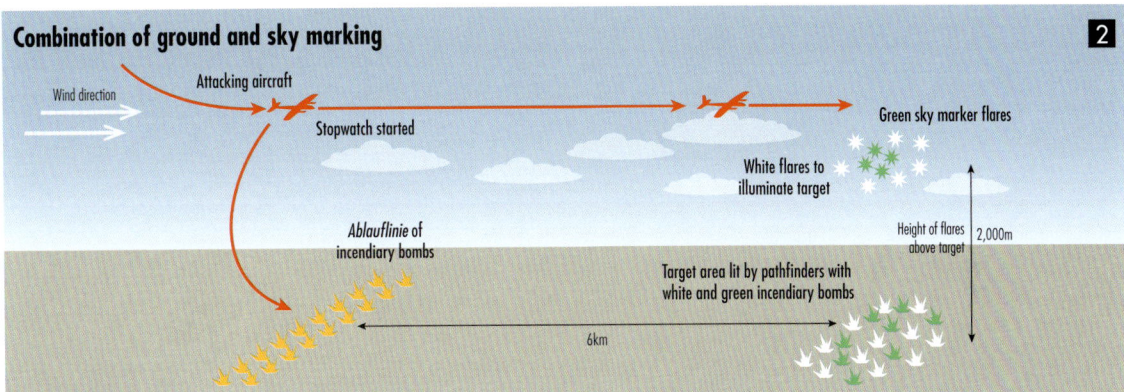
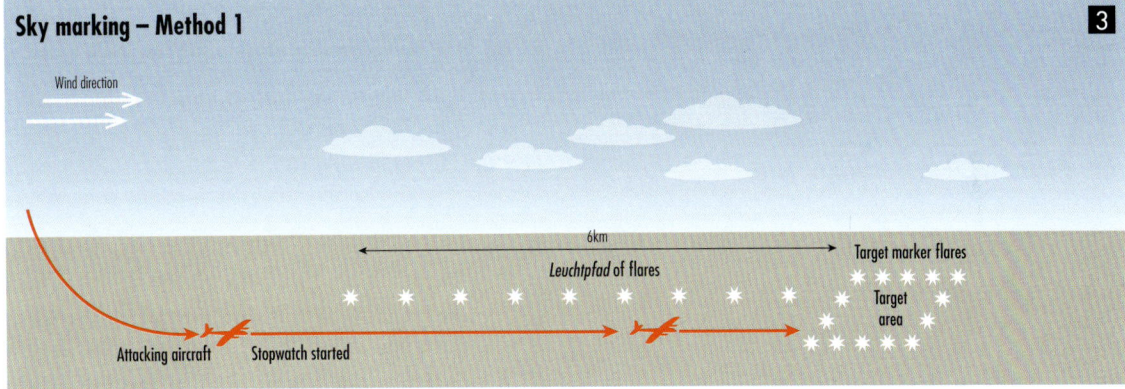
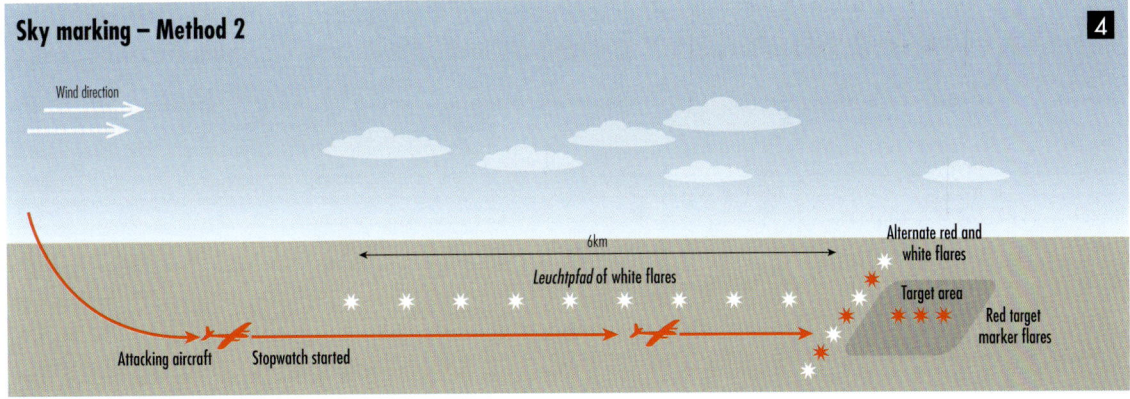

He 177A of 2./KG 100. The He 177 first flew in November 1940 but did not go operational until November 1943. Both KG 100 and KG 40 flew this type in *Steinbock*. (Author's collection)

Fw 190A-5 Jabo. An effective fighter-bomber, its use at night by I./SKG 10 was questionable as its effectiveness was minimal and inaccurate. (Author's collection)

Bomber employment

Compared to the last full night of the Blitz on 10 May 1941, the Luftwaffe's tactics were considerably different. On 10 May 1941, Luftflotte 3 reported at 2254hrs British time that the pathfinders of KGr 100 had dropped their bombs. From then until 0624hrs German time, when a Ju 88 of II./KG 54 released its bombs, London was subjected to a concerted and terrible air attack. The bombers attacked in two waves, with Luftflotte 3 reporting 291 attacking in the first wave and 67 in the second; the precise number committed by Luftflotte 2 is uncertain, but 571 bomber sorties were apparently flown that night – a number of other targets were also attacked that evening by single aircraft. Aircraft would take off individually, hence the attack lasting so long, unlike the daylight formation attacks of the Battle of Britain. In respect of pathfinding, in addition to KGr 100 with X-Verfahren, III./KG 26 was used with Y-Verfahren.

For *Steinbock*, the Luftwaffe adopted the RAF's bomber stream tactic, which meant attacks were more concentrated and, should crews and aircraft permit, would allow a second wave. However, unlike the RAF, aircraft would cross the French, Dutch or Belgian coasts at low

level, climb to cross the English coast to an altitude of 23,000ft or more and then attack the target at a shallow angle, allowing them (hopefully) to get away from the target and danger as quickly as possible. That was the theory – though practice during *Steinbock* for many crews was much more different.

Luftwaffe order of battle and strength for 20 January 1944					
Unit	Commander	Based	Aircraft	Strength	Serviceable
Stab./KG 2	Obstlt Karl Kessel	Soesterberg	Do 217	3	3
I./KG 2	Hptm Franz Schönberger	Eindhoven (Melun)	Do 217	35	35
II./KG 2	Maj Heinz Engel	Münster-Handorf	Ju 188	35	31
III./KG 2	Hptm Albert Schreiweis	Gilze-Rijen	Do 217	38	36
V./KG 2*	Hptm Kurt Heintz	Vitry-en-Artois	Me 410	27	25
Stab./KG 6	Obstlt Hermann Hogeback	Melsbroek	Ju 88	3	3
I./KG 6	Maj Helmut Fuhrhop	Chièvres	Ju 188	41	41
II./KG 6	Maj Hans Mader	Le Culot	Ju 88	39	39
III./KG 6	Maj Rudolf Puchinger	Melsbroek	Ju 88	41	37
II./KG 30**	Maj Ernst Pflüger	Eindhoven	Ju 88	36	31
1 & 2./KG 40***	Maj Karl Henkelmann	Châteaudun	He 177	15	15
Stab./KG 54	Obstlt Volprecht Riedesel Frhr zu Eisenbach	Marx	Ju 88	3	3
I./KG 54	Hptm Otfried Sehrt	Wittmundhafen (Juvincourt)	Ju 88	36	25
II./KG 54	Hptm Karl Palliardi	Marx (Laon/Athies)	Ju 88	33	33
I./KG 66	Maj Hermann Schmidt	Montdidier	Ju 88S/188	45	23
Stab./KG 76	Obtlt Rudolf Hallensleben	Couvron	Ju 88	5	4
I./KG 76	Maj Günther Schulz	Varrelbusch (Couvron)	Ju 88	33	31
I./KG 100****	Hptm Hans-Gotthelf von Kalckreuth	Lechfeld/Châteaudun	He 177	31	27
I./SKG 10	Maj Kurt Dahlmann	Rosières	Fw 190	25	20
Total				524	462
* V./KG 2 would be redesignated II./KG 51 1 March 1944 and recommence operations in April 1944					
** III./KG 30 commanded by Hptm Helmut Störchel would participate on this first night operating from St Trond, and joining II./KG 30 in March 1944; while I./KG 30 would join in May 1944					
*** 1./KG 40 was commanded by Hptm Bodo Mayerhofer, 2./KG 40 by Hptm Fritz Hoppe; 3./KG 40 was flying the Fw 200 and based in Norway					
**** It is believed that only 3./KG 100 commanded by Hptm Kurt Mayer was available on 20 Jan 44 with 15 aircraft. 2./KG 100 commanded by Hptm Herbert Dostlebe would join 3 Staffel early February 1944					

DEFENDER'S CAPABILITIES
Facing the enemy

Z Battery in action. This unusual system fired 3in. unrotated projectiles either singularly or in salvoes up to 20,000ft and was quite effective in scaring Luftwaffe bomber crews as they saw them approaching. (Author's collection)

The air defence of the United Kingdom was entrusted to Fighter Command which in 1943 was split to be Air Defence of Great Britain (ADGB) and the Second Tactical Air Force. It was initially commanded by Air Chief Marshal Sir Trafford Leigh-Mallory, formerly Air Officer Commanding (AOC) 12 Gp and then AOC 11 Gp, and based at RAF Bentley Priory. Leigh-Mallory handed over command to Air Chief Marshal Sir Roderic Hill, formerly AOC 12 Gp, in November 1943, just in time for *Steinbock*.

Air Chief Marshal Hill had four fighter groups under his command – 10 Gp at RAF Box in Wiltshire commanded by Air Vice-Marshal Charles Steele, 11 Gp at RAF Uxbridge in Middlesex commanded by Air Vice-Marshal Hugh Saunders, 12 Gp at RAF Watnall in Nottinghamshire commanded by Air Vice-Marshal Malcolm Henderson and 13 Gp at RAF Inverness commanded by Air Vice-Marshal Stanley Vincent. It would be 10 and 11 Gps which experienced the brunt of *Steinbock*'s attacks.

The RAF had a tried and tested defensive system, the so-called Dowding System, named after Air Marshal Hugh Dowding, Commander-in-Chief Fighter Command before and during the Battle of Britain, where early warning radar and the Royal Observer Corps fed hostile aircraft information to Sector Controllers who then fed it to the Fighter Command Filter Room, which then decided the defensive response, feeding it to Group HQ, then Sectors and finally the defences themselves. From 1941, Groups had their own Filter Rooms to take the pressure off Fighter Command and to reduce the length of the command-and-control chain. Furthermore, the introduction of Ground-Controlled Interception (GCI) radars, such as the Air Ministry Experimental System (AMES) Type 7, allowed controllers – unlike the Chain Home radars of the Battle of Britain, which faced away from the British coastline – to have a 360-degree view of the airspace around the radar to a distance of about 90 miles. These were both permanent and mobile based around the United Kingdom, and were known as 'happidromes' (codenamed after a 1943 comedy film and 1941 radio comedy programme; 'happidromes' could also be found at many British seaside resorts, a form of amusement arcade for visitors). By early 1944, other radar types were being added to the

Air Ministry Experimental Station (AMES) Type 7 Ground Control Interception (GCI) radar seen at RAF Sopley in Hampshire. Such radars gave a 360-degree view around the United Kingdom. (Author's collection)

GCI stations. For example, some AMES Type 11 radars, operating roughly 560–600 MHz, were deployed to counter enemy jamming; also, dedicated height-finding radars AMES Type 13 (3,000 MHz) were being introduced. The AMES Type 20 Mark I was being installed at Durrington (West Sussex), Sandwich (Kent) and Wartling (East Sussex) – this was a large 'nodding' height finder operating at 600 MHz.

The 3.7in. AA gun was Britain's primary heavy AA gun throughout World War II. It was roughly the equivalent of the German 88mm and American 90mm, but with a slightly larger calibre of approximately 94mm. Production began in 1937 and it was used throughout World War II in all theatres and even remained in use after the war. (Author's collection, courtesy of the late K. Wakefield)

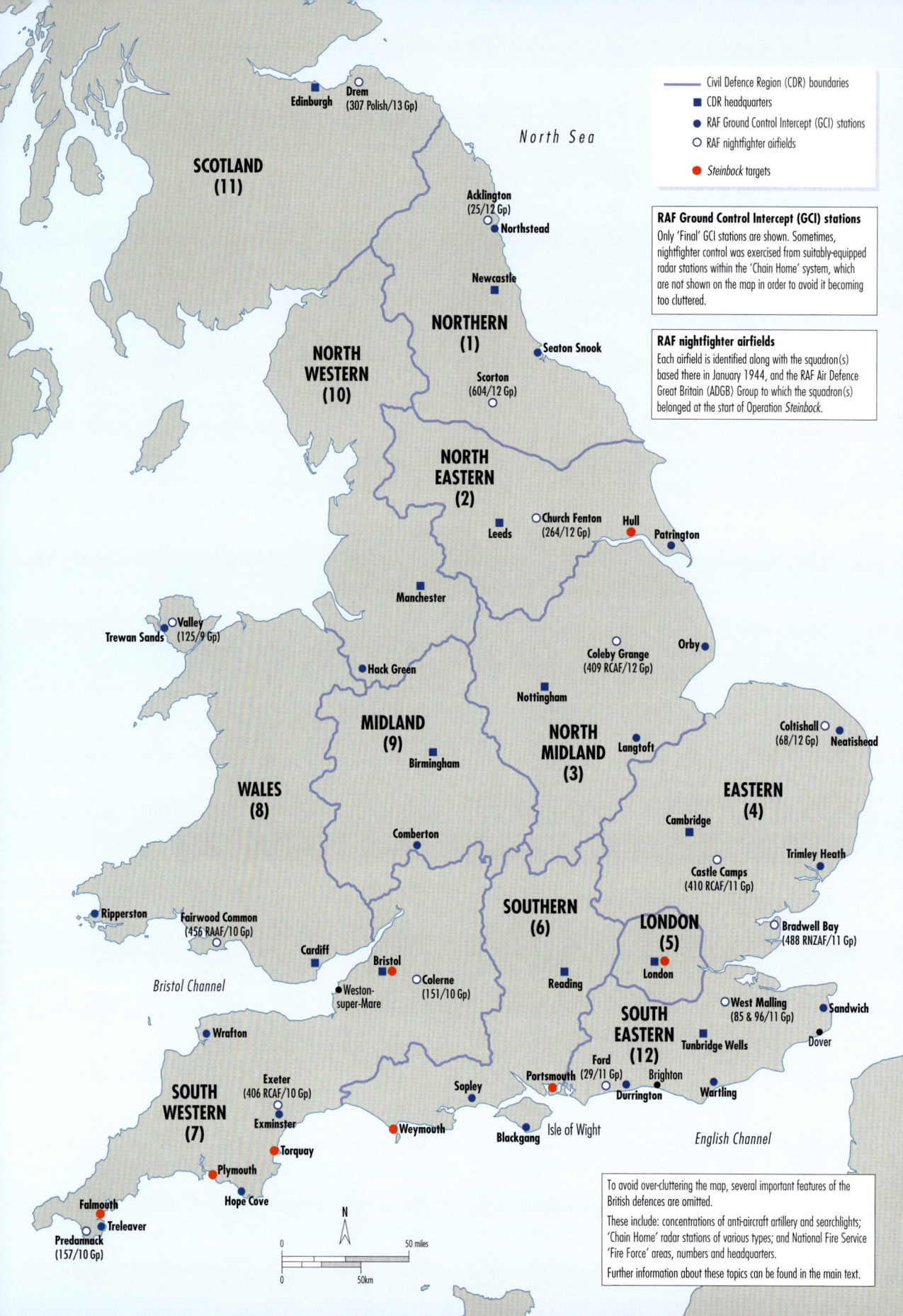

OPPOSITE MAP OF BRITISH DEFENCES

Furthermore, the first six AMES Type 21 radars were being sited at Sandwich, Neatishead (Norfolk), Trimley Heath (Suffolk), Wartling, Hope Cove (Devon) and Sopley (Hampshire). Plan position was provided by a fixed version of the Type 14 radar, with its larger aerial giving improved vertical cover, while height information was provided by the AMES Type 13 Mark II. It was clear that British radar was, by January 1944, much more advanced than that experienced by the Luftwaffe in the summer of 1940.

With London the main target for the Luftwaffe, it was the responsibility of the 1st Anti-Aircraft Gp (1 AA Gp) to defend it from the ground. With its HQ at Stanmore in Middlesex and commanded by Major-General Erroll Tremlett, it was responsible for the London Inner Artillery Zone (IAZ), which was later expanded to include Thames North and Thames South. The Operations Room was in the Brompton Road and controlled four Gun Operations Rooms (GORs) – 301 GOR at Stanmore, 320 GOR at Hastings, 329 GOR at Vange and 330 GOR at Chelmsford. London itself was split into three Gun Defended Areas (GDA) designated ZE for east (25 sites), ZW for west (14 sites) and ZS for south (29 sites). Each site contained a mix of heavy anti-aircraft guns (5.25in., 3.7in. Mk VI, 3.7in. static and 3.7in.mobile) and Z Batteries, a short-range anti-aircraft system which launched 3in. Unrotated Projectile 3 (UP-3) rockets either singly or multiple and which travelled at 1,500ft per second up to an altitude of 20,000ft. Effectively, this provided a ring of steel around the country's capital which left the approaches to and from London a hunting ground for RAF nightfighters. By March 1944, the IAZ had 30 5.25in., 57 3.7in. Mk VI, 198 3.7in. static and 26 3.7in.mobile guns at its disposal together with Z Batteries.

ADGB had 19 nightfighter or intruder units available to them of which all but five were equipped with the de Havilland Mosquito, these five being equipped with the Bristol

3.7in. battery in action. Such guns were both static and mobile. (Author's collection, courtesy of the late K. Wakefield)

A. Single-storey administrative and technical section.
B. Two-storey operations section.

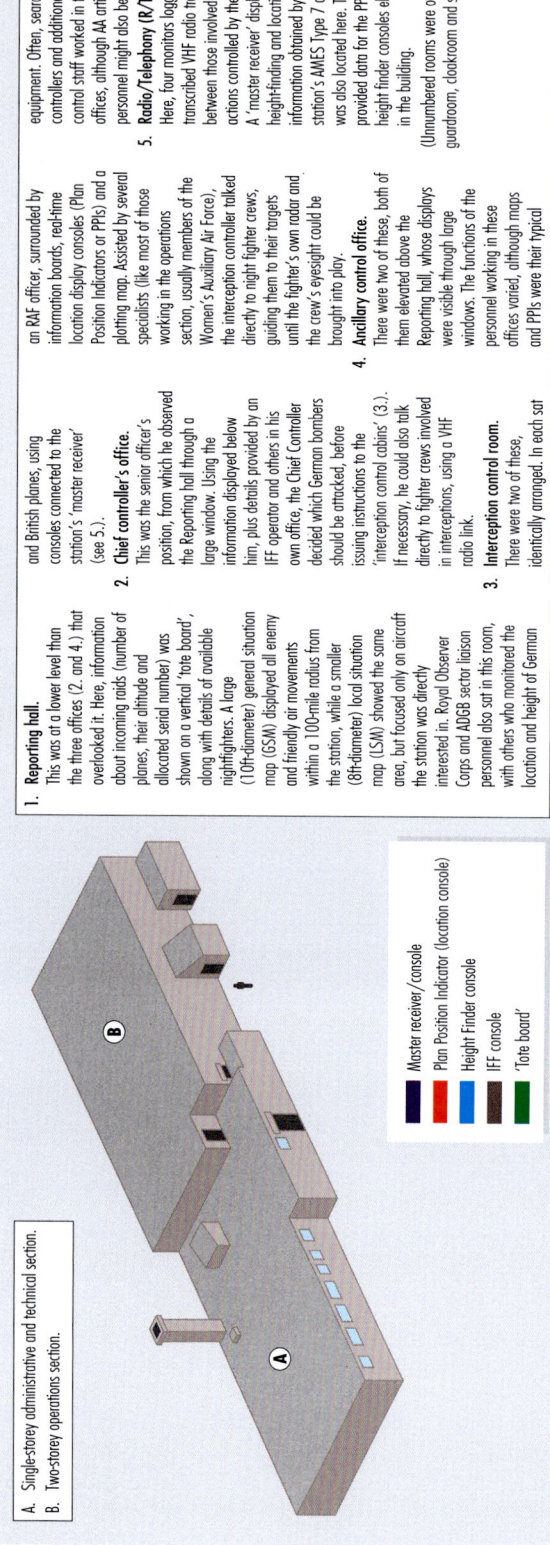

- Master receiver/console
- Plan Position Indicator (location console)
- Height Finder console
- IFF console
- 'Tote board'

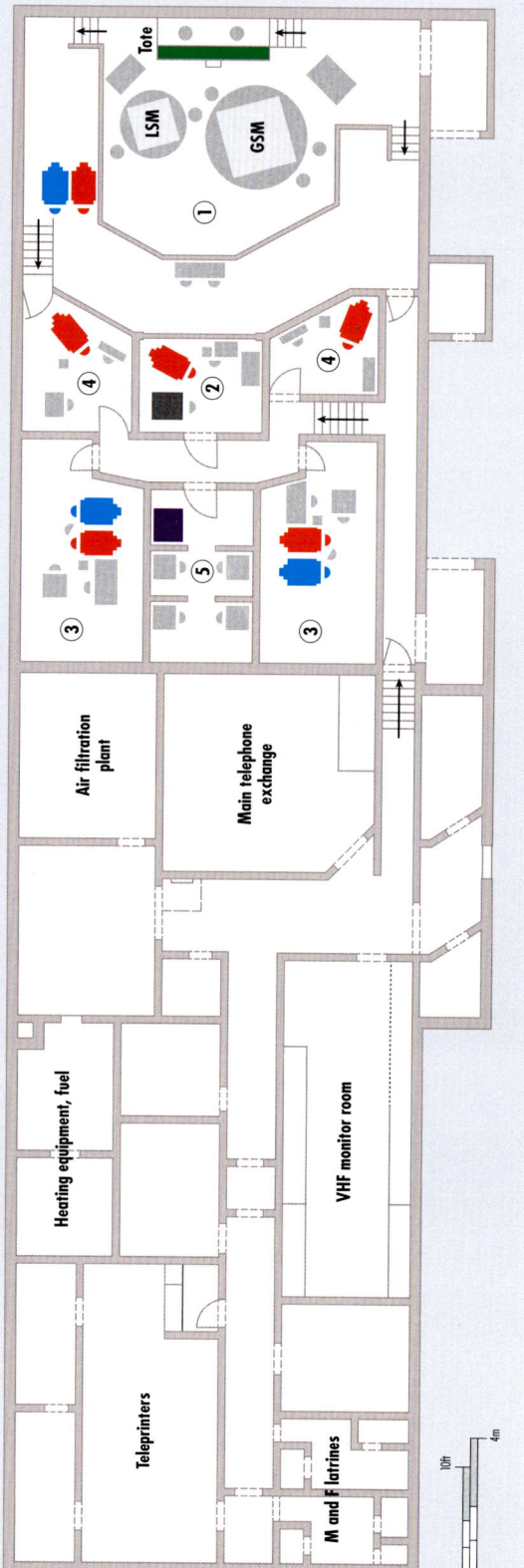

1. **Reporting hall.**
   This was at a lower level than the three offices (2. and 4.) that overlooked it. Here, information about incoming raids (number of planes, their altitude and allocated serial number) was shown on a vertical 'tote board', along with details of available nightfighters. A large (10ft-diameter) general situation map (GSM) displayed all enemy and friendly air movements within a 100-mile radius from the station, while a smaller (8ft-diameter) local situation map (LSM) showed the same area, but focused only on aircraft interested in. Royal Observer Corps and ADGB sector liaison personnel also sat in this room, with others who monitored the location and height of German and British planes, using consoles connected to the station's 'master receiver' (see 5.).

2. **Chief controller's office.**
   This was the senior officer's position, from which he observed the Reporting hall through a large window. Using the information displayed below him, plus details provided by an IFF operator and others in his own office, the Chief Controller decided which German bombers should be attacked, before issuing instructions to the 'interception control cabins' (3.). If necessary, he could also talk directly to fighter crews involved in interceptions, using a VHF radio link.

3. **Interception control room.**
   There were two of these, identically arranged. In each sat an RAF officer, surrounded by information boards, real-time location display consoles (Plan Position Indicators or PPIs) and a plotting map. Assisted by several specialists (like most of those working in the operations section, usually members of the Women's Auxiliary Air Force), the interception controller talked directly to night fighter crews, guiding them to their targets until the fighter's own radar and the crew's eyesight could be brought into play.

4. **Ancillary control office.**
   There were two of these, both of them elevated above the Reporting hall, whose displays were visible through large windows. The functions of the personnel working in these offices varied, although maps and PPIs were their typical equipment. Often, searchlight controllers and additional fighter control staff worked in these offices, although AA artillery personnel might also be present.

5. **Radio/Telephony (R/T) room.**
   Here, four monitors logged and transcribed VHF radio traffic between those involved in the actions controlled by the station. A 'master receiver' displaying height-finding and location information obtained by the station's AMES Type 7 antenna was also located here. This provided data for the PPIs and height finder consoles elsewhere in the building.

   (Unnumbered rooms were offices, guardroom, cloakroom and storage.)

OPPOSITE THE GCI 'HAPPIDROME'

Final GCI stations included AMES Type 7 radars (later supplemented by AMES Types 13 and 14), as well as at least one IFF (Identification, Friend or Foe) antenna, generators, offices and other structures. But their nerve centre was the operations block or 'Happidrome', a building which took its self-deprecating nickname from a wartime BBC radio comedy programme about a variety theatre ('The Happidrome') whose staff worked in a state of near-permanent chaos. In fact, by 1944, the staff in these facilities – among them, many women and experienced former pilots – generally cooperated with considerable skill and efficiency, processing data about incoming raids, to guide RAF nightfighters to positions from which their own airborne radars and direct observation allowed them to deliver close-range attacks on German bombers.
'Happidromes' at GCI stations were built from brick and concrete to a standard design, although there were occasional differences in internal layout. The external view and floor plan shown here are based closely on illustrations contained in Colin Dobinson's *Building Radar: Forging Britain's Early-Warning Chain, 1935–1945* (English Heritage/Methuen 2010), an essential source for anybody who wants to find out more about the subject.

Beaufighter Mk. VIF. The Beaufighter was fitted with AI Mk. VII. However, there were a number of different variants of Mosquito, some of which (the intruders) were not fitted with AI.

Mosquito variants January 1944	
Mk. II	Day/night long-range fighter and intruder. AI Mk. IV and V
Mk. IV	Day/night bomber
Mk. VI	Day/nightfighter-bomber/intruder/long-range fighter
Mk. XII	Nightfighter conversion of Mk. II with AI Mk. VIII 'Thimble Nose'
Mk. XIII	Nightfighter with AI Mk. VIII 'Thimble' or 'Bull Nose'
Mk. XVII	Nightfighter conversion of Mk. II with AI Mk. X in 'Bull Nose'

Each aircraft carried a crew of two – pilot and Nav/Rad. The Beaufighter had a top speed of around 330mph and was armed with four 20mm cannon and six .303 machine guns. It could operate at 30,000ft altitude and had a range of 1,540 miles. The latest Mark of Mosquito was the NF Mk. XVII, which had a top speed of around 370mph, was armed with four 20mm cannon, had a ceiling of 30,000ft and range of 1,700 miles; both the Beaufighter and Mosquito were therefore formidable and superior adversaries for the Luftwaffe. Assuming that each ADGB nightfighter squadron had a strength of 16 aircraft, in theory around 300 highly capable nightfighters which could be easily and quickly replaced were waiting for *Steinbock*. In reality, a number of squadrons were converting to the Mosquito or being upgraded to better variants of Mosquito. A good example of this was 219 Sqn – commanded by former Battle of Britain pilot Wg Cdr Archibald Boyd – which had been operating Beaufighter Mk. VIFs in North Africa and, at the end of January, arrived at RAF Woodvale, where it would start converting to the Mosquito XVII, moving to RAF Honiley on 15 March 1944 and then to RAF Colerne on 26 March 1944. For most of *Steinbock*, 219's crews were training on its new Mosquito and the first kill, a Ju 88 probably destroyed by Plt Off Desmond Tull and his Nav/Rad Plt Off Peter Cowgill, came on 25 May 1944, by which time *Steinbock* was all but over. Of the five Beaufighter squadrons on the ADGB's Order of Battle at the start of *Steinbock*, 68 Sqn would have converted to the Mosquito Mk. XVII by July 1944 and 125 Sqn would have converted to the Mk. XVII by March 1944. 406 Sqn would have converted to the Mk. XII by August 1944, 409 Sqn would also have converted to the Mk XII by May 1944 and finally, 604 Sqn would have converted to the Mk. XIII by April 1944.

What gave the RAF nightfighter crews a better chance of success was that most nightfighters carried AI radar. The AI Mk. IV had been around since the start of the night war and was

A predictor as seen here was used to determine when AA shells exploded – seen here in use by 76th Heavy AA Regiment at Portbury, Somerset. (Author's collection, courtesy of the late K. Wakefield)

responsible for the destruction of the first German bomber on the night of 19 November 1940, when Flt Lt John Cunningham of 604 Sqn (and who by *Steinbock* was commanding 85 Sqn) shot down a Ju 88A-5 of 3./KG 54 south of Chichester. Its maximum range was around three and a half miles and initially the minimum range was 1,000ft, but this reduced to around 400ft as it was further refined. It was replaced by the Mk. V, which was quickly replaced by the Mk. VIII. It had a similar range to the Mk. IV, but its beam was so sharply focussed that it easily avoided ground reflection even at low level. However, it could only see targets directly in front of the antenna, unlike the Mk. IV, which could see all in front of the aircraft. This was sorted by mounting the radar dish on bearings which allowed it to rotate and thus see more. The Mk. X used a helical scan instead of a spiral. The radar antenna was spun around a vertical axis through an entire 360 degrees ten times a second, with the transmitter switching off when the antenna was pointed back towards the aircraft. This provided a 150-degree scan in front of the aircraft. As it spun, the antenna slowly nodded up and down to provide altitude coverage between +50 and -20 degrees. It had a maximum range of six miles and a minimum range of 300ft. However, it was only just arriving on RAF squadrons and thus only Wg Cdr Keith Hampshire's 456 Sqn and Wg Cdr John Cunningham's 85 Sqn were equipped with the Mosquito XVII, which was the variant fitted with AI Mk. X. Also known as SCR-720, it was so advanced for its time that it continued to be used by Meteor, Vampire and Venom jet nightfighters after the war until replaced by the AI Mk.21.

Air defence of Great Britain nightfighter/night intruder units 1 January 1944			
Unit	CO	Based	Aircraft Type
10 Gp (Air Vice-Marshal C. R. Steele)			
125 Sqn	Wg Cdr J. G. Topham	Valley	Beaufighter VIF
151 Sqn	Wg Cdr G. H. Goodman	Colerne	Mosquito XIII/VI
157 Sqn	Wg Cdr J. A. Mackie	Predannack	Mosquito II/VI
406 Sqn	Wg Cdr R. C. Fumerton	Exeter	Beaufighter VIF
456 Sqn	Wg Cdr K. M. Hampshire	Fairwood Common	Mosquito II/VI/XVII
11 Gp (Air Vice-Marshal H. W. L. Saunders)			
29 Sqn	Wg Cdr R. E. X. Mack	Ford	Mosquito XII/XIII
85 Sqn	Wg Cdr J. Cunningham	West Malling	Mosquito XII/XVII
96 Sqn	Wg Cdr E. D. Crew	West Malling	Mosquito XII/XIII
410 Sqn	Wg Cdr G. H. Elms	Castle Camps	Mosquito XIII
418 Sqn	Wg Cdr D. C. S. MacDonald	Ford	Mosquito VI
488 Sqn	Wg Cdr R. C. Haine	Bradwell Bay	Mosquito XII/XIII
605 Sqn	Wg Cdr B. R. O'Bryen Hoare	Bradwell Bay	Mosquito VI
Fighter Interception Unit	Wg Cdr C. H. Hartley	Ford	Mosquito XIII
12 Gp (Air Vice-Marshal M. Henderson)			
25 Sqn	Wg Cdr C. M. Wight-Boycott	Acklington	Mosquito II
68 Sqn	Wg Cdr D. Hayley-Bell	Coltishall	Beaufighter VIF
264 Sqn	Wg Cdr W. J. Alington	Church Fenton	Mosquito XIII
409 Sqn	Wg Cdr J. W. Reid	Acklington	Beaufighter VIF
604 Sqn	Wg Cdr M. H. Constable-Maxwell	Scorton	Beaufighter VIF
13 Gp (Air Vice-Marshal S. F. Vincent)			
307 Sqn	Wg Cdr M. Lewandowski	Drem	Mosquito II/VI

CAMPAIGN OBJECTIVES
The start of the vengeance campaign

Generalfeldmarschall Hugo Sperrle visiting an unknown unit, early 1944. Sperrle's part in *Steinbock* was very much secondary to that of Peltz's. (Author's collection)

In respect of *Steinbock*, historians are lucky in that the original order signed by Hermann Göring and dated 3 December 1943 survived the war and clearly states his aim, 'To avenge the terror attacks of the enemy I have decided to intensify the air war over the British Isles by means of concentrated attacks on cities and especially industrial centres and ports.' (See the full letter on p. 30.) In actuality, London was the city targeted while from April 1944, ports such as Hull, Bristol, Falmouth, Weymouth, Plymouth and Portsmouth were also targeted in an attempt to disrupt the build-up for the invasion of Normandy.

On paper, Luftflotte 3, commanded by 58-year-old Generalfeldmarschall Hugo Sperrle, was given the task of carrying out *Steinbock*. However, due to the high profile of the campaign amongst the higher echelons of the Nazi Party, the bomber assets – commanded by former General der Kampfflieger, then Fliegerführer England and finally from September 1943 Kommandierender General IX Fliegerkorps Generalmajor Dietrich Peltz – bypassed Sperrle and reported direct to Göring.

Sperrle, Oberbefehishaber Luftflotte 3, had held this position since February 1939. He had joined the Imperial German Army in 1903 and following the outbreak of World War I, had transferred to the Luftstreitkräfte, first as a reconnaissance observer and then as a pilot. He was injured in a crash on 23 February 1916 while with Flieger Abteilung 42, still an observer but with the rank of *Hauptmann* (Captain). He would recover to command the observer school at Köln and ended the war as Kommandeur der Flieger for 7 Armée, which operated in the Alsace. However, unlike Göring (who was a fighter pilot), he did not receive any major award such as the Pour le Mérite (also known as the Blue Max), but did receive the Hausorden von Hohenzollern with Swords. He remained in the Reichswehr after the war and by the time the Nazis came to power, he had been promoted to Generalmajor. He was selected to command the Legion Condor in the Spanish Civil War from November 1936 to October 1937, after which he took command of Luftwaffengruppenkommando 3, the predecessor of Luftflotte 3, with the rank of Generalleutnant.

OPPOSITE MAP OF GERMAN AIRFIELDS AND NAVIGATIONAL AIDS

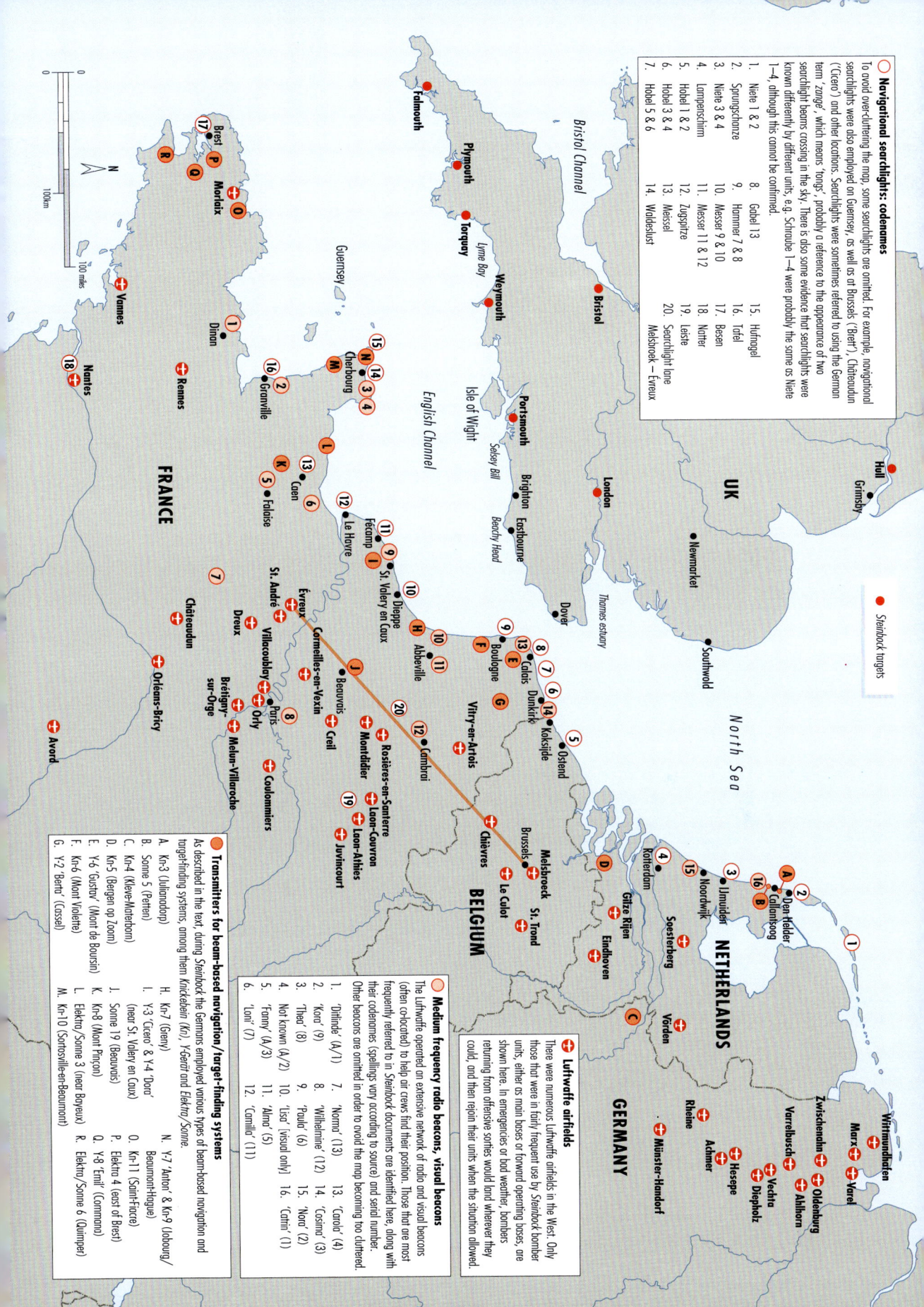

General Peltz (2nd from left) visiting KG 6 during *Steinbock*. 4th from left is Kommodore Oberst Hermann Hogeback. (Author's collection)

Maj Rudolf Puchinger, Kdr III./KG 6 was an Austrian pilot who started his operational career with 8./LG 1 in spring 1941. He took command of the Staffel in May 1942, which in September 1942 became 8./KG 6. He was awarded the Ritterkreuz in January 1943, took command of III./KG 6 in August 1943 but was killed in action on 13 June 1944. (Author's collection)

After the outbreak of war, by which time Sperrle had been promoted to General der Flieger, Luftflotte 3 remained on the Western Front and as a result, was heavily involved in the Battle of France, Battle of Britain, Blitz, Baedeker Blitz and the Battle of the Atlantic, and by now was headquartered in Paris. Luftflotte 3 was also responsible for fighter units there to counter the RAF going on the offensive in 1941, and from 1942, the USAAF. He would receive the Ritterkreuz in May 1940 and was finally promoted to Generalfeldmarschall in July 1940.

Due to the failures of Luftflotte 3 in the Battle of Britain and afterwards, it is believed that he fell out of favour with Göring, unlike his fellow commander in Luftflotte 2 in 1940, Generalfeldmarschall Albert Kesselring. Visibly, both Generalfeldmarschalls could not have been more different – Kesselring was nicknamed 'Smiling Albert', while photos of Sperrle portray him as a gruff, pompous, unsmiling and overweight man. However, it is believed that Sperrle did have support from Adolf Hitler, hence a reason for his longevity in post. He remained in post until being replaced by Generaloberst Otto Dessloch on 23 August 1944, his removal being due to Luftflotte 3's failures following the Allied invasion of Normandy. Luftflotte 3 would then be renamed Luftwaffenkommando West a month later and would be commanded by Generalleutnant Alexander Holle until he was replaced in November 1944. Neither Dessloch nor Holle lasted anywhere near Sperrle's six years and six months as a Luftflotte commander, of which five years saw him commanding forces in wartime, and even by the Battle of Britain, he was by far the Luftwaffe's most experienced air commander.

Sperrle delegated the operational and tactical nuances of *Steinbock* to 29-year-old Generalmajor Dietrich Peltz, who had a meteoric career and was one of the most influential German bomber officers of the war. He joined the Reichswehr in 1934 but the following year transferred from the Army to the Luftwaffe. He completed his flying training and joined I./Stukageschwader 162 (I./St.G 162) in April 1936. He would fly 102 missions over Poland and then France with 1./St.G 76 but then converted to the Ju 88, joining Stab./KG 77. He would be awarded the Ritterkreuz on 14 October 1940, and on 30 October 1940 it is believed he took command of 6./KG 77. He was promoted to Hauptmann in March 1941, taking command of II./KG 77 on

11 March 1941. He flew his 200th mission on 12 July 1941 but was posted to the *Verbandsführerschule für Kampfflieger* (school for bomber pilots) in Foggia, Italy at the end of September 1941. He would be awarded the Eichenlaub (oak leaves) on 31 December 1941, promoted to Major in July 1942, and then took command of the Verbandsführerschule für Kampfflieger when it moved to Tours in France, the unit then becoming I./KG 60 in September 1942. At the end of the year, he was promoted to Oberstleutnant and appointed as General der Kampfflieger aged 28. In March 1943, he would become Angriffsführer England with personal responsibility for air attacks on mainland Britain. He would be promoted to Oberst and received the Schwerter in July 1943. He would then be promoted to Generalmajor and took command of IX Fliegerkorps four months prior to when *Steinbock* was due to start.

IX Fliegerkorps had a number of experienced and well-decorated officers commanding many of its units at the start of and during *Steinbock*. Ritterkreuz holders included Obstlt Karl Kessel (KG 2), Hptm Kurt Heintz (V./KG 2), Maj Helmut Fuhrhop (I./KG 6), Hptm Johann Mader (II./KG 6), Maj Rudolf Puchinger (III./KG 6), Obstlt Volprecht Riedesel Freiherr zu Eisenbach (KG 54), Maj Hermann Schmidt (I./KG 66), Obstlt Rudolf Hallensleben (KG 76), Hptm Johann Thurner (6./KG 6) and Hptm Kurt Maier (3./KG 100). Obstlt Hermann Hogeback (KG 6) had also been awarded the Eichenlaub; Thurner, Maier and Riedesel Freiherr zu Eisenbach would also receive this award later. Two of these Ritterkreuzträger would be killed during *Steinbock* (Heintz and Fuhrhop), as would Hptm Dietrich Puttfarken of 5./KG 51, who did not join his Staffel until March 1944, and Fw Otto Heinrich (3./SKG 10). Three would be killed over Normandy (Thurner, Mader and Puchinger) and two would be killed before the end of the war (Hallensleben and Riedesel Freiherr zu Eisenbach).

Hptm Johann Thurner (right), a highly experienced bomber pilot, had been awarded the Ritterkreuz as a Leutnant with 9./KG 55 in August 1941. He took command of 6./KG 6 in September 1943 and command of I./KG 6 in March 1944. He was killed in action on 11 June 1944 and awarded the Eichenlaub to the Ritterkreuz posthumously. (Author's collection)

Obstlt Rudolf Hallensleben (centre), Kommodore KG 76, during an award ceremony for the Ritterkreuz to Ofw Georg Hanke, formerly of II./KG 76 but at this time instructing with 10./KG 76. Hallensleben had flown operationally with 2./KG 76 from the start of the war and had become a Kommodore of KG 76 in January 1943. He was awarded the Ritterkreuz in October 1943 but was killed in a strafing attack by American fighters on 19 April 1945. (Author's collection)

3 December 1943

1. To avenge the terror attacks of the enemy I have decided to intensify the air war over the British Isles by means of concentrated attacks on cities and especially industrial centres and ports.
2. For the intensification of the war against England, the following additional units are to be committed:
   a. From Luftflotte 2: KG 30, KG 54, KG 76 each with two Gruppen (of which one Gruppe only temporary).
   b. From re-equipped units: II./KG 6 (Ju 88), I./KG 100 (He 177), I./KG 51 (Me 410).
3. All units are to be concentrated against targets making use of all the experience gained during the previous month's operations against England. The operations are to be carried out in a manner and frequency depending on casualties and replacements so that the fighting strength of the units remains absolutely unimpaired. This is in view of the necessity to maintain a permanent defensive capability against the ever-present threat of an attempted enemy invasion in the west.
4. Operational readiness and the stocking-up of the units earmarked for the operations are to be speeded up by all possible means so that the operation can begin at the end of the full-moon period in December. The detailed measures necessary for this are to be ordered by the Quartermaster General.
5. The necessary preparations, especially those of the ground organisation, are to be initiated without delay. Advanced airfields are to be used for the attacks only. The units' main and reserve bases are to be moved back. In so far is necessary, use is to be made of airfields in the Reich territory with the agreement of the commander Central Area. On the airfields themselves the aircraft are to be widely dispersed and parked well away from the runways; they are to be given shrapnel protection so as to nullify the effect of anticipated enemy bombing attacks. In addition, a dummy occupation is to be made of the advanced airfields which are not to be used.
6. Particular attention is to be paid to the selection and preparation of bombs. In general, in all attacks, 70% of the load is to be used for carrying incendiary bombs; of the high explosive bombs first and foremost the heaviest types (1,000kg) are to be used with the 'England Mixture' (Trialen) and air mines. Smaller types are to be used only to make up the loads. Experts from the office of the Director of Air Armaments, Engineer General [Ernst] Marquardt and [Walter] Marienfeld, are to be available to give advice on this.
7. HQ IX Fliegerkorps is to report to Luftflotte 3 as soon as possible:
   a. Its intentions, stating the targets for December and January.
   b. Its intentions for their execution in general.
   c. The state of Flak and fighter defences to the C-in-C Luftwaffe operations staff.
8. Express attention is drawn to the need for especial secrecy for all preparations. Only those persons who have an absolute need to know of them are to be briefed. In each case the scope of the brief is to be restricted to the absolute minimum necessary. Special directives will follow on the security of the transfer operations. C-in-C Luftflotte 2 has already been informed verbally.

(signed)
Göring
Reichsmarschall of the Greater German Reich and C-in-C Luftwaffe

THE CAMPAIGN
The Luftwaffe's last sustained offensive

On 20 January 1944, Generalmajor Peltz arrived at Châteaudun and briefed the He 177 crews of I./KG 40 and I./KG 100 (in actuality, just 1 and 2./KG 40 and 3./KG 100). Peltz said that Germany was approaching an important and strenuous phase of the war – they had suffered the destruction of their home towns by British bombs without retaliating, but now the time for retribution had arrived and as soon as weather conditions allowed, large-scale attacks on England would commence and he called upon the crews to 'pull their weight and if necessary to fly two sorties a night'.

He 177A-3 of 2./KG 100 coded 6N+SK. This aircraft was named Susi after the aircraft's individual code letter S. (Author's collection)

Headed for Germany from the Mediterranean is a Ju 88A of 9./KG 76. This unit did not take an active part in Steinbock as it would be converting to the Arado 234 jet instead. (Author's collection)

OPPOSITE MAP OF ROUTES AND TARGETS DURING THE *STEINBOCK* RAIDS

Peltz neither mentioned dates or targets but the following night, a two-wave attack was carried out against London on a scale which had not been seen since 10 May 1941. *Steinbock* had begun.

What surprised the RAF after the attack was the widespread dispersal of Gruppen and Geschwader taking part afterwards:

> The units … were based at airfields from Brittany and south of Paris to western Germany but even so, in order to prevent any concentration of aircraft from being observed, the unit bases in France were further dispersed in small batches on different airfields. A few hours before the attack was due to begin, the units which were to take part were quickly concentrated on a few airfields in northern France and in one case an airfield in Holland. After the raids-in many cases directly from the second sortie-aircraft were again to disperse to other airfields.

First night

The first wave consisted of around 227 aircraft, with the attack lasting from 2040hrs to 2233hrs. The lead aircraft crossed the coast at Beachy Head flying at around 10,000ft, followed by the main force, which made landfall between the Isle of Wight and North Foreland in Kent. After crossing the coast, they fanned out over south-east England at heights from 7,000ft to 22,000ft. However, bombing was assessed by the British as wildly inaccurate despite the use of navigation aids and flares, and it was thought afterwards the small number of pathfinders contributed to this failure. The target area was a 4-sq-km zone around Waterloo in central London which would be marked by incendiaries. EGON and

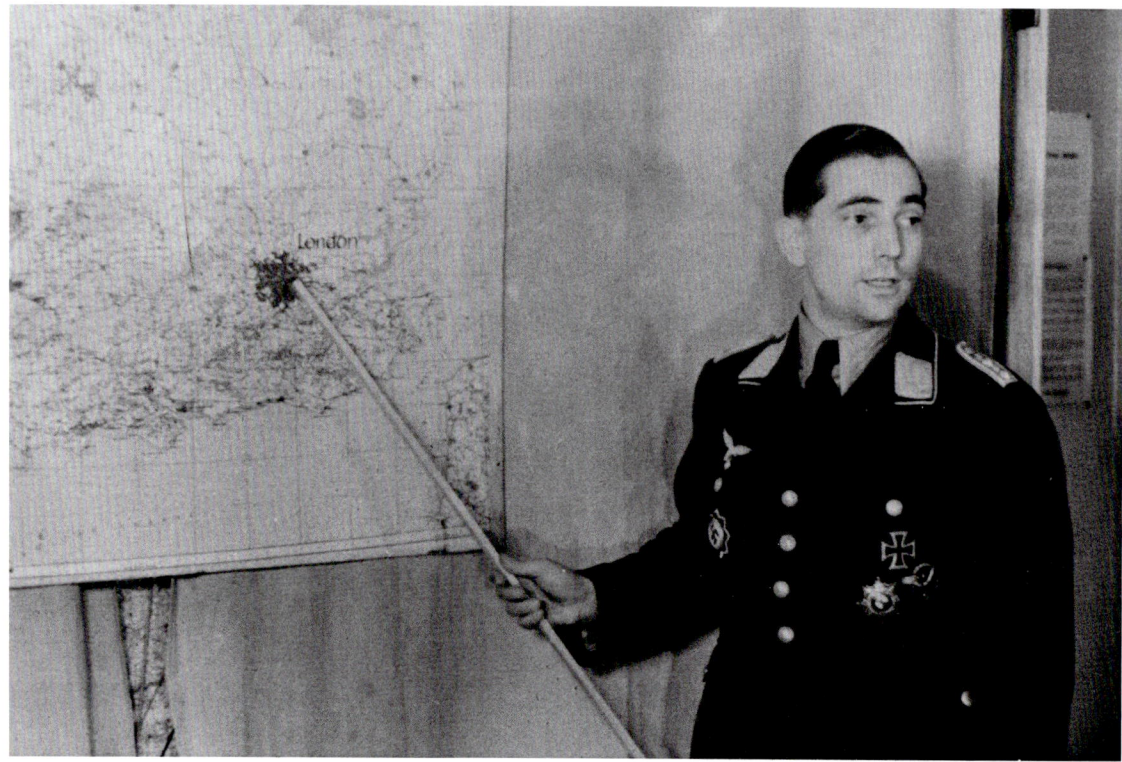

Hptm Kurt Seyfarth of Stab./KG 2 briefing an attack on London, Soesterberg, early 1944. Originally a transport pilot, Seyfarth joined KG 2 in March 1943. He would be awarded the Ritterkreuz in September 1944 and survived the war. (Author's collection)

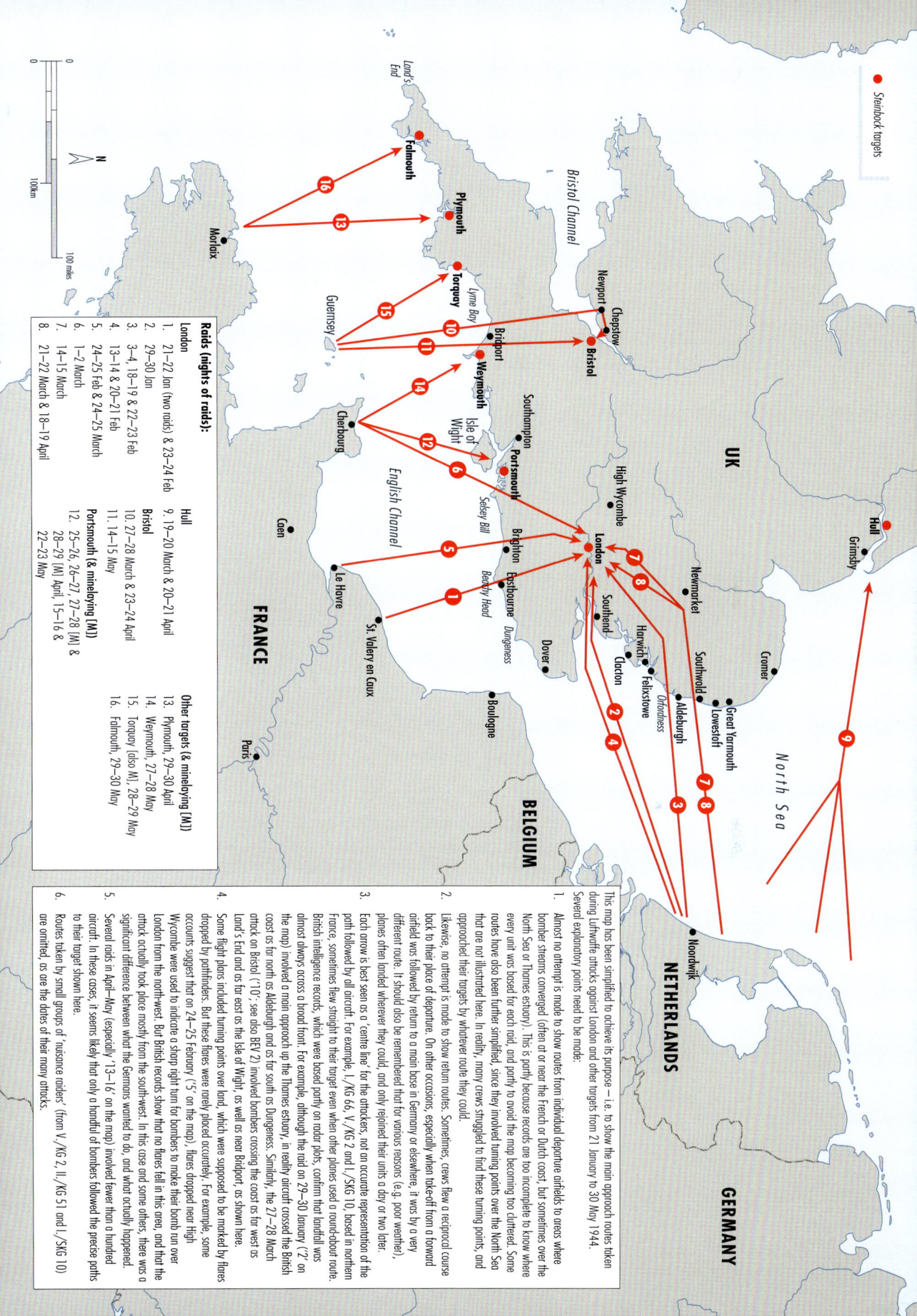

He 111 fitted with X-Gerät as indicated by the three masts. Using a main approach beam with three cross beams, which with a manual timer checked the aircraft's speed over the ground and then provided automatic bomb release, it was similar to the Knickebein system which by using a powerful transmitter, an intersection of two narrow beams produced an accurate position fix. Positioning such an intersection over the target allowed crews to bomb blindly with some accuracy. (Author's collection)

Y-Verfahren was used while Hptm Walter Schmitt, Staffelkapitän of 2./KG 66, carried a captured Gee system (known as Hyperbel or Truhe Gerät) in his Ju 188.

The second wave was of around 220 aircraft and crossed the coast between Selsey Bill in West Sussex and North Foreland at around 0415hrs, and although the weather conditions had worsened, this attack was slightly more successful than the first.

The Home Security assessment of the attacks was blunt:

> The attack was conducted in two phases. In the first phase, only 14 aircraft succeeded in reaching London and in the second 13. As a result there was considerable spill, mainly in south-eastern England; in Kent alone over 100 minor incidents occurred. In London, the bulk of the incidents were south of the River. A considerable number of unexploded bombs and incendiary bombs were dropped and considering the scale of effort, the results were very poor and compared unfavourably with those of the attack on Birmingham on 29–30 July 1942.

It was reported afterwards that four fires were started by the bombing, 74 civilians were killed, 12 were seriously wounded and 91 Key Points were affected, considerably less than the Birmingham attack.

More worryingly to Peltz were German losses. Despite having 35 Do 217s, 20 Me 410s, 20 Fw 190s, 30 He 177s and 170 Ju 88/188s available to them that night, losses were heavy. The bombers dropped much Düppel (window or chaff), so much so that controllers using older types of GCI had difficulties in directing nightfighters, especially as there were too many targets to cope with despite flying 96 nightfighter sorties. Nevertheless, an incredible 16 Ju 88s, two Ju 188s, eight He 177s, one Fw 190, one Me 410 and four Do 217s were lost either to British defences or crashing to or from the target either due to technical problems or combat. In terms of the human cost, 74 aircrew were killed or missing, 15 captured and eight wounded or injured on the two raids this night.

In June 1944, the Luftwaffe's 8th Abteilung wrote the following about the first night of *Steinbock* which was part of the way to the truth if not optimistic:

> Pathfinder aircraft operated successfully for the first time during this attack. Their value was however lessened by the small number of aircraft employed. In all subsequent raids, larger pathfinder formations were in operation.
>
> The favourable weather conditions prevailing during the attack by the first wave, together with successful target marking and flare illumination enabled our aircraft to drop the majority of their bombs in the target area within the limited time allowed for the attack. During operations by the second wave, however, 10/10ths cloud conditions were encountered so that concentration of effect was not possible. In view of the size of the target it can nevertheless be assumed that most of our bombs fell in the London area.

Enter the Griffon

As to the blooding of the He 177 as a conventional bomber, the He 177 attack was led by Ritterkreuz winner Hptm Kurt Maier, Staffelkapitän of 3./KG 100, but it was not a good start. 1./KG 40 lost two aircraft over Britain or in the Channel, which were flown by Oblt Karl Waterbeck and Oblt Helmut Botterbrodt respectively, while one flown by Ofw Hugo Fleischer crashed near Rouen on the return with the deaths of all of the crew. From 2 Staffel, Lt Rolf-Heinrich Melcher crashed near Amy in France (all but one of the crew being killed), while two more aircraft from I./KG 40 were also believed to have crashed after suffering engine fires. A single He 177A-3 was lost by 3./KG 100 when Oblt Hans-Werner von der Dovenmühle lost control and crashed at Les Grandes-Ventes 15km south of Dieppe, killing all five on board; his was the only loss from I./KG 100.

Karl Waterbeck had recently celebrated his 29th birthday and had been in military service since April 1936. He had flown 47 transport flights over Poland, Denmark, Norway, France and Belgium with the Ju 52 unit 2./KGrzbV 1 before converting to the Fw 200, and from January 1941 until October 1943, flew 82 operational flights with 3./KG 40. He would be promoted from Feldwebel to Oberleutnant in 1943, receiving the *Ehrenpokal* (Honour Goblet) in March 1943 and the *Deutsches Kreuz* in Gold (German Cross in Gold) in November 1943 having already received the *Frontflugspange* (Operational Mission

WO Howard Kemp (back row, 2nd from left) and Flt Sgt Jim Maidment (back row, 3rd from right) of 151 Sqn, who shot down the first He 177 to crash on British soil on the first night of *Steinbock*. Both would be killed in action on 11 April 1944 in combat with German twin-engined fighters over the Bay of Biscay. (George Kelsey)

Oblt Rudolf Haschke, Stafelkapitän of 2./KG 6, who failed to return on the first night of *Steinbock*. It is believed that his Ju 188 must have come down in the sea – there were no survivors from his crew. (Author's collection)

Clasp) in Gold in September 1941; he would be promoted to Hauptmann posthumously. His He 177 was the first to crash on British soil, having been intercepted by a Mosquito of 151 Sqn flown by WO Howard Kemp with Flt Sgt Jim Maidment as his Nav/Rad. Kemp had turned to investigate a cone of searchlights when the Nav/Rad picked up a target ahead at a range of two miles. On approaching the He 177, the German pilot pulled into a tight evasive turn and the Mosquito lost contact but regained it shortly afterwards:

> WO Kemp decided to attack and dropped back, coming up dead astern five degrees below when he opened fire with a short burst. As he did so he noticed some projectiles between the port engine and fuselage and assumed them to be bombs–they almost filled the available space. The burst took immediate effect and a violent explosion was seen on port wing–a white flash with orange round the edges accompanied by a shower of sparks. There was no return fire. A white swastika was visible on the rudder in the light of the explosion. E/a [Enemy aircraft] then skidded violently to port and went down in a spiral dive which was too steep for Mosquito to follow. It was last seen going down burning with exhaust stubs on starboard side still glowing and subsequently found crashed near Haslemere.

The He 177 had entered a steep dive; the bombload, two SC2000 bombs carried externally, was jettisoned and three crew baled out. Waterbeck attempted to force-land at Whitmore Vale near Hindhead in Surrey but crashed and the wreckage caught fire. He and gunner Gefr Johannes Conrad were killed but amazingly the tail gunner, Ogefr Werner Döge, managed to crawl out of the wreckage without serious injuries. Two of those who were captured, Ofw Georg Six (*Bordmechaniker*) and Ofw Erwin Mirbach (*Bordfunker*), had flown with Waterbeck on Fw 200s over the Atlantic for the previous two years and, under interrogation, reported that they had only been posted to Fassberg in November 1943 for conversion to the He 177 and, after just over a month, had joined 1./KG 40 at Châteaudun; this was the crew's first operational flight with the He 177.

After capture, this crew gave the RAF an interesting insight to the mission:

> For the first attack, six or seven crews of I./KG 40 and two crews from 2./KG 100 were called for briefing. The No 7 [Before leaving Fassberg on 20 December 1943, I./KG 40 had its unit lettering over-painted (but retaining F8+) and a numeral painted over the cross, this aircraft being 7, and was commented on by the RAF when the wreckage was inspected – Author], one of the first aircraft which took part in the sortie, was bombed up with two 2000kg High Explosive (HE) bombs slung externally which were to be dropped over the north-west suburbs. The aircraft were to meet up near Châteaudun and were carefully timed to cross the English coast and arrive over the target at exactly the same time. "7", the first aircraft to take off, was airborne at 1950hrs and orbited the airfield until 2015hrs by which time the remainder of the attacking force had assembled. The French coast was crossed over marker searchlights near Dieppe . "7" was ahead of ETA and the pilot circled for a few minutes over the Channel before crossing the English coast near Eastbourne at a height of 6500m. Düppel was liberally used …

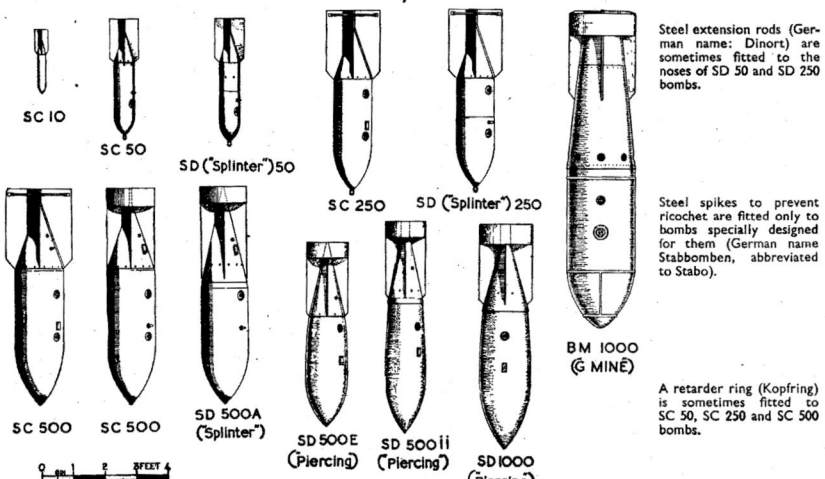

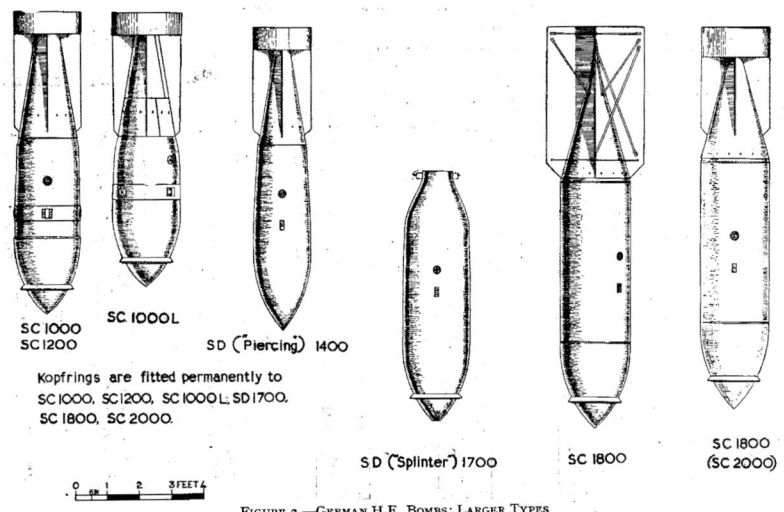

Types of bombs used by the Luftwaffe in *Steinbock*. They ranged from the SC10 incendiary which were dropped in their hundreds of thousands in *Steinbock* to the standard SC250 and SC500 bombs, 1,000kg air mines and the SC1800, the latter bomb being capable of considerable devastation but which could only be carried externally by certain aircraft types. (Author's collection)

The other serious loss, Helmut Botterbrodt, was a pre-war seaplane pilot, flying with 1./Küstenfliegergruppe 106 before becoming an instructor, then transport pilot and then joining 1./KG 40. An equally experienced but less decorated pilot, he and his crew disappeared over the Channel; the reason why has never been determined despite considerable research by his son after the war.

In the second attack that night, Ofw Alfred Billing of 2./KG 40 was shot down into the Channel by Fg Off Christopher Nowell of 85 Sqn. Nowell and his Nav/Rad Flt Sgt Fred Randall had just damaged a Ju 88 when they were vectored onto another contact:

> He obtained contact at four miles range 20 degrees at two o'clock on target flying straight about 30 degrees off to starboard. Pilot turned inside and closed range quickly to 2,000ft then to 1,500ft. Pilot identified e/a as a Ju 88 [sic] and opened fire producing a big explosion and causing the aircraft to dive away out of control and in flames. Operator reports that he then saw, falling from the burning aircraft, objects which appeared to be two of the crew baling out.

Hptm Kurt Heintz (right), Kdr V./KG 2, who was killed on 22 January 1944 when his Me 410 crashed at Lydd. He was the first Ritterkreuz winner to be killed during *Steinbock*. (Author's collection)

Billing and three of his crew were killed while two were captured. Again, one of those captured gave an insight into the second He 177 sortie that night:

> Five or six crews of I./KG 40 took part in the second sortie, two of these belonging to 1 Staffel, had taken part in the first raid. At the briefing the target for this second attack was stated to be Government buildings in London and crews were told that Me 410s were to mark the target by means of incendiary bombs forming a large square which would be easily visible from a considerable height. The four corners of the square were to be marked with green and white flares. Not quite so much attention was paid to concentration on attack; the aircraft were to take off at short intervals and fly individually to the targets. ETA over London was to be 0512hrs and his aircraft was carrying two 1800kg and two 1000kg bombs which were to be released with the aid of the Lotfe 7D bomb sight. From this sortie the aircraft were not to return to Châteaudun but were to land at Rheine [Germany]. Owing to the failure of the electrical circuit and engine trouble, this crew was obliged to jettison their bomb-load and to turn back. While over the Channel, orders were given to bale out and two of the crew who did so were captured; the aircraft crashed into the sea near Hastings …

Of note, both Lt Rolf-Heinrich Melcher and Billing were flying former 3./KG 4 He 177s, this unit being re-formed as I./KG 100 in October–November 1943, so were probably on loan to 2./KG 40. As further proof of the difficulties these crews faced that night, Oblt Hugo Müller of 1./KG 40 suffered engine failure on the first sortie and returned early, and then he and his crew were forced to bale out of their He 177A-3 near Châteaudun due to an engine fire on the second sortie. From an He 177 aircrew point of view, 21 were killed or missing, six captured and one injured that first night of *Steinbock*, but more importantly, four of those pilots who were killed were highly experienced. Ofw Alfred Billing was an experienced Fw 200 pilot. Thirty-one-year-old Ofw Hugo Fleischer of 1./KG 40 would be awarded the

Ehrenpokal after his death, but the deaths of Oblt Karl Waterbeck (who would be promoted to Hauptmann posthumously) and Oblt Helmut Botterbrodt were serious for I./KG 40 and all of these losses adversely affected future operations, as it appears that I./KG 40 only flew two more *Steinbock* missions before being withdrawn back to Fassberg.

In terms of effect, the first night of *Steinbock* had been a failure, with a loss rate of 10% – British defences and German inexperience, inaccuracy and naivety were to blame for this. It was clear to the Luftwaffe that such losses would soon become unsustainable, and an immediate result was no more double attacks in one night. Losses of both experienced and inexperienced aircrew would seriously affect German bombing effectiveness for the remainder of *Steinbock* and afterwards over Normandy. One casualty in particular was Ritterkreuz winner Hptm Kurt Heintz, Gruppen Kommandeur of V./KG 2. British intelligence noted:

> It has now been established that the Me 410 which crashed at Lydd in Kent at 0450hrs on 22 January 1944 belonged to Stab V./KG 2. Both crew members, one of whom was a Hauptmann with the Ritterkreuz, were killed and it is possible that this aircraft was one of the pathfinders which were to light up the target for the He 177s.

Heintz had flown from the start of the war with II./KG 51, 8./KG 51, 9./LG 1 and II./KG 40, and had been on operations since the start of the war and was awarded the Ritterkreuz as early as October 1942, when he had flown 300 missions. His Bordfunker Stfw Otto Runge, who was killed with him, had also been awarded the Deutsches Kreuz in Gold in September 1942 with 9./LG 1 and had presumably been flying with Heintz for some time. In the wreckage, the RAF found a briefing note which gave the course to be followed that night:

1. Base [Vitry] to peak of climb
2. Peak to climb to beacon Liesa (St-Valéry-sur-Somme)
3. Liesa to English coast
4. English coast to Ablauflinie
5. Cross Ablauflinie glide attack and release bombs
6. Fly to 51.39N 02.52E [midway between Southwold and The Hague]
7. 51.39N 02.52E to Ostend
8. Ostend to base

Next attack

It would be another six days before a further attack, thanks mainly due to bad weather and the high losses on the first night of *Steinbock*. It is believed that just 16 Me 410s of V./KG 2 and two Fw 190s of I./SKG 10 attacked London on the night of 28 January 1944. Fw Hermann Bolten of 14./KG 2 recorded he was acting as pathfinder for an attack on London, while Oblt Rudolf Abrahamczik, Staffelkapitän of 14./KG 2, reported taking off five minutes after Bolten and that he encountered heavy Flak over London. Bombing was again scattered over East Anglia and South-East England 'but they accomplished almost nothing'. RAF nightfighters were not as lucky this night, with only Sqn Ldr Alastair Parker-Rees of 96 Sqn claiming an Me 410 damaged over Kent at 2235hrs. Furthermore, Sub Lts Tom Blundell and Jack Parker, flying with 85 Sqn, failed to return from a patrol, reporting that they were baling out following an engine fire; neither were ever found.

There would be one more *Steinbock* attack before January 1944 was over, on the night of the 29th. Just one wave of around 285 aircraft this time and despite a heavy AA barrage, 343 fires were reported, and 41 civilians killed and 116 seriously injured in London.

Ogefr Erich Schiml, a Bordfunker with 2./KG 6, whose diary gives us a good account of the early *Steinbock* raids. He was killed in action on 22 March 1944, which is why his diary ended suddenly. (Rick Back)

Nightfighters were not as successful, with just two Ju 88s claimed destroyed by 68 and 410 Sqns and one, claimed by Fg Off Stan Hibbert of 96 Sqn, as a probable. Hibbert's claim was an unusual one as he successfully attacked a Ju 88A-14 of 5./KG 6 flown by Lt Hans Berstecher, who apparently lost control and gave the order to bale out. Two crew did so, being captured near Biddenden in Kent, but the pilot then regained control, flying back to St Omer where the remaining two crew baled out, the Beobachter being killed at Lottingen to the west of St Omer when his parachute failed to open; Berstecher would be killed with a new crew returning from an attack on London on the night of 3 February 1944. Of the attack that night, the Luftwaffe, again optimistic about the effect but truthful about the problems, later wrote:

> Despite unfavourable weather conditions, the use of Y and EGON equipment enabled our aircraft to carry out a powerful attack. Due to ground organisational difficulties, however, caused by the long absence of our bombers from large scale operations and consequent servicing deficiencies, a number of aircraft intended for this attack failed to take off.

Despite the lack of RAF success, the Germans still lost 13 Ju 88s, two Ju 188s, an He 177 and a Do 217, with another 53 aircrew killed and six captured. The most senior loss was 29-year-old Hptm Helmut Schüttke, Staffelkapitän of 9./KG 6, another officer who had been in the Luftwaffe since 1936 but who only had limited current combat experience, having left 1./KG 55 in May 1940 and joined III./KG 6 in the Mediterranean in August 1943; he had also flown with the Legion Condor with 2.K/88, where he was awarded the Spanish Cross in Gold with Diamonds. Both Oblt Rudolf Abrahamczik and Fw Hermann Bolten of 14./KG 2 were flying that night, both taking off at the same time, and the latter again reporting heavy Flak over London. The Luftwaffe later reported that II./KG 51 and I./SKG 10 had carried out 121 *Störangriff* (harassing attack) sorties during the first six nights of *Steinbock*.

Peltz had already stated that he was concerned by many of his crews having a lack of experience, especially against British targets and that they would come up against both British technological and weapons superiority. Losses from 21–29 January were heavy and would be slow to replace, while the long awaited He 177 fell far short of what was expected of it. In fact, it was so poor that on 28 January 1944, Adolf Hitler, talking to Generaloberst Günther Korten, the Luftwaffe Chief of Staff, is reported as saying:

> One gets the impression that once again the He 177 has suffered 50% breakdowns. They cannot even get as far as London. This heap of c**p is obviously the biggest load of rubbish that was ever manufactured. It is the flying Panther [the Panther tank suffering from poor reliability] and the Panther is the crawling Heinkel!

While 1 and 2./KG 40 were being used over London, at the same time II./KG 40 was now forced to fly from Bordeaux-Mérignac, over France, to attack targets at Anzio in Italy

An He 111 of III./KG 26 fitted with Y-Gerät indicated by the single large mast. Y-Gerät used a single beam to provide track guidance together with a distance-measuring facility. The beam was produced by a ground transmitter which broadcast three directional signals, while a second ground station would measure the bomber's distance out along the beam by sending a signal that triggered a transponder in the aircraft and sent a signal back. This allowed the ground station to measure the distance to the aircraft, and when the aircraft's distance matched that of the target distance, instructions were sent for bombs to be released. (Author's collection)

following the Allied invasion on 22 January 1944. Seven He 177s were lost attacking Anzio and Nettuno between 23 and 26 January, an eighth being lost in a convoy attack on 1 February 1944. II./KG 40 therefore played no part in *Steinbock*, especially as it appears that I./KG 40 only flew two more *Steinbock* missions before being withdrawn to Fassberg. The first was the night of 29 January 1944 operating from Münster in Germany, and saw Oblt Günter Kampf and three of his crew being killed when their He 177 crashed near Schwege. Then, in the early hours of 5 February 1944, Oblt Hugo Müller of 1./KG 40 recorded having taken off from Châteaudun at 0255hrs to attack London, after which he landed at Soesterberg in Holland at 0542hrs. From then on, I and II./KG 40 did very little until the Allied invasion of Normandy on 6 June 1944. The only He 177 unit left was 3./KG 100, which was now joined by Hptm Herbert Dostlebe's 2./KG 100 (it appears that Hptm

Oblt Rudolf Abrahamczik (centre) of 14./KG 2 following the award of his Ritterkreuz at the end of February 1944. In the background is an Me 410A-1 of 14./KG 2. Abrahamczik was originally a Do 217 pilot with KG 2 and would end the war flying Me 262 with 2./KG 51. (Author's collection)

Beaufighter XVF of 29 Sqn. By the time of *Steinbock*, most Beaufighter squadrons had converted to the Mosquito, 29 Sqn being no exception. It was then based at RAF Ford in West Sussex. (Author's collection)

Oberbefehlshaber der Heeresgruppe B, Generalfeldmarschall Erwin Rommel, visiting I./KG 6 at Chièvres, early 1944 . He is seen here with Maj Helmut Fuhrhop who would be killed in action at the end of February 1944. (Author's collection)

Leonhard Knapp's 1 Staffel never participated in attacks on Britain in 1944) and would continue flying sporadic attacks against London, carrying out at least five attacks in February 1944 and then four more in March and April 1944, the last being the night of 18 April 1944.

New month, no change

Steinbock's February attacks started on the night of the 3rd. Crews were put on standby earlier that day and the first attacks were carried out by 16 Me 410s of V./KG 2 and 19 Fw 190s of I./SKG 10. Oblt Rudolf Abrahamczik and Fw Hermann Bolten of 14./KG 2, recorded taking off at 2005hrs and 2006hrs respectively, the former reporting heavy Flak over London while the latter was used as a pathfinder. V./KG 2 reported dropping 12 x SC500, 30 x SC250 and four SB70 bombs, landing back without incident, albeit 2./SKG 10 lost Lt Friedrich Engel and 3./SKG 10 Uffz Hermann Wurster, both of whom were killed crashing back in France.

A second more intensive wave of attacks took place after midnight and is best described by Ogefr Erich Schiml, a Bordfunker with 2./KG 6. He would be shot down and killed on 22 March 1944 and his diary was found on his body; his account of the first mission of February 1944 gives a good insight as to what happened:

First breakfast at 0030hrs-operational rations with real coffee. Our new Staffelführer, Lt Hans-Friedrich Lenkeit [he had replaced Oblt Rudolf Haschke, who was killed on the first night of *Steinbock*] was not allowed to take part, he wishes us all good luck. At 0100hrs we dressed ourselves up in our Channel suits going off at 0115hrs for briefing. Oblt Karl von Manowarda [Staffelkapitän of 1./KG 6] is our formation leader. Briefing as usual-our target is Seeschlange [Sea Serpent-code name for London]. Take off was to be at 0355hrs but at 0345hrs we were still looking for our "Caesar" [Ju 188E-1 3E+CK]. We finally found her and were the last but one to take off at 0415hrs in foul weather. Today a second gunner flew for the first time as fifth man. Seemed fairly unintelligent to me but, thank heavens, he is only helping out. Load 2 x AB1000 and 10 Phosphorous High Explosive (Br.C 50). Ofw B and Uffz H [Uffz Ernst Holst] fail to start. Ostende (Zange-directional searchlight) and Flak star shells over the sea. First turning point is at 4000m. First attack by nightfighter noticed by Rudi—we finally curved away from the blighter. Arrived at the coast—Düppel. Over the target at 0540hrs. Bombs away at 0543hrs. An astonishing amount of Flak today and a number of searchlights coming through the 6–8/10ths cloud. Many fires and explosions. Once a fine bundle of Flak bursts passed us by (damned close). With all speed out of the muck. We had thought we had already come too far and were to the right of the airfield. Then we got an astonishing QDM [magnetic bearing to a station] and there we were. Everyone circling around the airfield. We waited and made a smooth landing. The Flak was still firing away at nightfighters. Report to Intelligence Officer and home to bed.

The Luftwaffe reported sending 235 bombers on the second wave that night, of which 210 made it to London. They initially described defences as being weak and that the attack as a whole was satisfactory but later admitted:

> Inaccurate target marking resulted in a loss of concentration and numerous bombs falling outside the target area. Enemy nightfighter defences were particularly strong.

Fw Günther Parge of 4./KG 6 flew actively throughout *Steinbock* and then over the Normandy beaches. He would survive the war. (Author's collection)

Bombs were widely spread as far as Gloucestershire and little major damage was done or for that matter terror inflicted, with 31 civilians killed and 88 injured, of which 16 were killed in London with another 45 injured. Losses were 12 aircraft failed to return, with another three either crashing on take-off or landing. Aircrew casualties were 56 killed and one injured; no aircraft crashed on mainland UK and no aircrew were captured this night.

For the next nine days, the Luftwaffe both attempted and achieved very little, with attacks being carried out by V./KG 2 and I./SKG 10. Surviving logbooks show just four Störangriff against London, the last being the night of 12 February 1944 when nine Fw 190s and 16 Me 410s attacked London between 2100 and 2106hrs; the British assessment was scathing:

> Five long-range bombers and 10 fighter-bombers crossed the coast between Hythe and Hastings and operated over Kent, Sussex and Essex for about half an hour. Three reached the Greater London Area. None of the incidents merits special mention …

Ogefr Erich Schiml in his diary shows that there was little operational flying after 4 February – in fact, there was quite a bit of socialising. They moved from Chièvres in Belgium to Ahlhorn in Germany on 9 February, but then moved back on 11 February for an attack on London on the night of 13 February:

> There is a balloon going up tonight. Leaving at 1645hrs. Briefing 1700hrs. Operation *Seeschlange* with 2 x AB1000 and 5 x Brand C.50. It is going to be a big thing again. A combined attack. We are flying. Had to break off twice as the rev counter showed only 2400 but then it reached 2700 and we were off–the last aircraft. In consequence, we fly with 1.2 boost and a short cut to the target. Our compass out of order, we strayed, returning home on emergency compass and landed at the third attempt. Two Do 217s fell down on the airfield–then a nightfighter came. The devil of a blaze and monster firework display on the perimeter. Take-off 1930hrs target 2100hrs landing 2200hrs.

Sqn Ldr Geoff Warnes of 263 Sqn, who was responsible for the destruction of a 3./KG 2 Do 217 in daylight near Gael in Brittany on 11 February 1944. Warnes would be shot down by Flak and ditched in the Channel on 22 February 1944. Seen in difficulties, another pilot baled out to help him but both failed to survive. The 'Fellowship of the Bellows' was the nickname of 263 Sqn. (Author's collection)

Hptm Mathias 'Teddy' Schwegler, Kommandeur of Verbandsführerschule/ KG 101. This unit flew the occasional attack during *Steinbock*. Schwegler first became operational with KG 51 in November 1939 but would be killed in action on 18 April 1945. The photo clearly shows the eidelweiss emblem of KG 51. (Author's collection)

V./KG 2 was also involved with Fw Hermann Bolten of 14./KG 2, describing it as a '*Grossangriff*' against London, while Uffz Franz Wachtler, also of 14./KG 2, reported dropping a *Spezialbombe* (SB)1000 bomb. The SB1000 was the maximum an Me 410 could carry and just about fitted into the bomb bay. Once dropped, this Luftmine's descent was slowed by a drogue parachute and the lateral blast effect, due to its thin casing, was considerable.

It is interesting to note that the crash of two Do 217s at Chièvres and the appearance of a nightfighter clearly illustrates another threat to the Luftwaffe – that from RAF intruders. For example, the day before, a Do 217 of 3./KG 2 was transferring from Vannes in daylight only to be shot down at Josselin in southern Brittany not far from the airfield at Gael. In addition to crew, it was carrying two groundcrew and was en route to Eindhoven. Sqn Ldr Geoff Warnes DSO DFC of 263 Sqn explained what happened:

> I was leading the squadron at zero feet in loose line abreast with myself to port. At 1457hrs we were flying east about five miles south of Gael airfield when I saw a Do 217 approaching to port at about 150ft. I called my section to follow and turned toward the e/a which turned away from me to the north, then to the east and south. The e/a took evasive action in gentle turns at zero feet at more than 300 IAS. I fired short bursts at various ranges and deflection. At first I got strikes only on the wing. Then a dull glow appeared in the centre section and the e/a pulled sharply to 1,000ft. I closed to 200yds and fired a long burst into it which made pieces fly off. I saw the crew of six bale out. Their parachutes opened as they left the e/a. The e/a then crashed with a remarkably large explosion. There was return fire from the dorsal position of the e/a. One explosive shell entered the leading edge of my starboard tail plane causing minor damage.

The pilot, Beobachter and Bordfunker baled out uninjured and hence their names are unknown. The gunner and

Mosquito NF XVII of 604 Sqn. This squadron would have converted from the Beaufighter to the Mosquito by April 1944, so played a minor part in *Steinbock*. (Author's collection)

Sqn Ldr Dean 'Red' Somerville (left), seen here as a Wg Cdr with 409 Sqn with his Nav/Rad Fg Off G. D. Robinson, who shot down the Ju 88A flown by Uffz Konrad Fisahn of Einsatzstaffel Verbandsführerschule/ KG 101 on the night of 13 February 1944. (Author's collection)

one of the groundcrew were wounded but another groundcrew member, Uffz Bruno Fiedler, was killed.

I./KG 2 and III./KG 2 recorded the loss of three aircraft over the Continent on 13 February 1944, with amazingly no apparent crew casualties despite what Ogefr Schiml might have thought. The two at Chièvres were probably due to Flt Sgt Frank Cassidy and his Nav/Rad Flt Sgt Charles Stickley of 605 Sqn, who claimed to have destroyed an unidentified aircraft over Chièvres at 2205hrs:

> When the Mosquito was about to open fire, the e/a crashed and burst into flames about 100yds short of the runway and continued to burn throughout the patrol. This e/a is claimed as destroyed as it was considered that the imminent attack of the intruder caused it to crash ...

Cassidy then attacked a second aircraft as it landed but made no claim as he was not sure he had damaged it.

As well as losses over the Continent, the attack on the night of 13 February saw another nine aircraft being lost, with another 33 aircrew killed and two captured. Six lost came from KG 6 and more worryingly for Peltz, two more were from the pathfinder unit I./KG 66, essential crews for successful future attacks. Curiously, another aircraft lost was a Ju 88A of Einsatzstaffel Verbandsführerschule/KG 101 flown by Uffz Konrad Fisahn and believed to have been shot down by Sqn Ldr Dean Somerville of 410 Sqn, the Ju 88 breaking in two and crashing off Clacton (it was also claimed by a number of AA units). KG 101 was a training unit based at Tours in France and commanded by the experienced Hptm Mathias 'Teddy' Schwegler, so why it had been committed to the attack that night with the effect that was intended is unknown, but it might be an indication of shortages of aircraft and crews and a need for operational experience. Again, the effect of the attack that night was assessed by the British as follows:

> About 100 long-range bombers made landfall between North Foreland and the Harwich/Orfordness area; probably 15 reached London, the remainder operating over Essex and south-eastern England. Activity lasted about two hours. There were clusters of incidents on the north side of the [Thames] Estuary … A considerable proportion of bombs were incendiaries but the fire situation amounted to only 14 medium and 18 small mostly in East Anglia. Casualties in London totalled one fatal and six serious and the whole country seven fatal, 11 serious and two missing believed killed.

It must have been clear to the Luftwaffe that despite their optimism, the efforts being made were clearly not having the desired results.

Change of fortunes – February 1944

The Luftwaffe was noticeable by its absence for the next four nights but returned with a vengeance on the night of 18 February 1944, with the RAF reporting 175 aircraft being involved (of which 120 operated over land) and the Germans 200 of which 184 made it to London, including Uffz Franz Wachtler of 14./KG 2, who again reported dropping an SB1000 on London.

Post-attack analysis that night stated there were 480 fires in London and 24 outside, and that 182 civilians lost their lives. Ogefr Schiml and his crew had a non-event of a night. After the briefing at 1800hrs had clarified that their target was London and the bombload four SC500 bombs, their Ju 188's engines failed to achieve the requisite revolutions for take-off, so they taxied back. 'Off to the hut by car. This sortie soon reached its undistinguished finish,' Schiml wrote.

Losses were unusually light that night, with three lost during the attack, one crashing on take-off and three crashing on return. A further two from 3./KG 54 were shot down by Flt Lt Bob Kipp and Fg Off Pete Hulotsky of 418 Sqn on an intruder mission to infiltrate the returning bomber streams. He shot down the Ju 88s flown by Uffz Heinrich Framing and

Maj Helmut Fuhrhop's Ju 188A of I./KG 6 after its crash-landing, 19 February 1944, which was mentioned in Erich Schiml's diary. With no casualties and the destruction of German records for 1944, the diary is the only proof of this crash-landing. (Author's collection)

Uffz Rolf Backofen near Juvincourt as they were returning from London, killing both crews. His were the only claims by nightfighters that night but why, at last, the bombers had been more successful cannot be deduced. However, as the Luftwaffe's records from 1944 are incomplete, it is probable that more aircraft were written off. Schiml in his diary for 19 February wrote:

> The Kommandeur [Maj Helmut Fuhrhop] made a belly landing. Weber [Uffz Ernst Weber] and the Staffelkapitän [Lt Hans-Friedrich Lenkeit] landed elsewhere. Holst [Uffz Ernst Holst] had an engine fire and landed at Melsbroek.

Two nights later, the Luftwaffe was back again with another major attack, with between 165 and 200 crews attacking. One of those involved was Ogefr Schiml:

Fw Günther Parge of 4./KG 6 being greeted by General Peltz on 21 February 1944, this photograph appearing in the German press afterwards. (Author's collection)

> Preparations in the afternoon for a fresh sortie. Let's hope we pull it off this time. We came early to take off and got off without incident at 1918hrs. Came to the first control point Rotterdam with searchlight cones and Flak star shells. Came correctly to the turning point Nora.

Ju 88A-4 evades rockets over London, 20 February 1944

On the evening of Sunday, 20 February 1944, approximately 165 bombers from several different Kampfgeschwader took part in the sixth major *Steinbock* attack against London. Twelve different Gruppen took part, including 15 Fw 190s from I./SKG 10.

Aircraft took off in a staggered sequence using a beacon at Noordwijk in Holland, with the He 177s of I./KG 100 and Ju 88s of I./KG 54 in the lead. The first wave made landfall near Southend, flew across north London before making a left-hand turn to begin its bombing run in a west-to-east direction. Subsequent aircraft were reported as crossing the coast in a loose pattern between Harwich in Essex and Hythe in Kent. Targets were south of the River Thames, apparently within a 1.5 by 2.25-mile rectangle south-east of Waterloo railway station. The target area was to be marked by I./KG 66 pathfinders, using red target-marking flares. By *Steinbock* standards, the raid achieved quite a high standard of concentration and caused a reasonable amount of destruction. Although many bombers failed to find their target, the British recorded 110 aircraft, of which 65 were identified over London, dropping 106 tonnes of bombs on the capital. German claims were much higher; they said that 171 aircraft reached the target area and that 247 tonnes of bombs were dropped.

According to British sources, the raid was met with intense AA fire and nightfighters. 23,685 rounds of heavy (mostly 3.7in.) AA ammunition were fired, as well as 536 rounds of light (mostly 40mm) ammunition. In addition, 471 UP-3 3in. rockets were fired, normally salvoes from various Z Batteries. Lt Wolfgang Fritz, a pilot with Stab/KG 54 who would be shot down and taken prisoner over Somerset on 27 March 1944 during an attack on Bristol, was overheard after capture talking about these rockets: ' [Rocket AA fire] ... is harmless. You can see the discharge and know where it will come. You see a sort of tail coming up from below. It is true that it looks frightfully dangerous in the air. There are about fifty points of burst in a bunch, but you know where it is ... I just keep out of the way of the AA rocket guns in Hyde Park and drop my bombs ... It would be crazy to fly over them. I don't fly over them but always skirt them. At any rate I make a large curve where the fifty points of burst are.'

In about two-thirds of cases studied by the British, German pilots reacted to UP-3 fire by changing course, sometimes quite violently, either on seeing the flash of the rocket launch or as the rockets ascended to the altitude at which they were set to detonate. Even in those cases where evasive action was taken only at the last moment, as the first rockets exploded, bombers were usually able to place themselves several hundred yards outside the danger area by a sharp and immediate change of course.

During the attack shown, on 20 February 1944, the Luftwaffe would lose one Ju 188, two Do 217s and four Ju 88s in action, with a Ju 188 crashing on take-off for the attack. Twenty-two aircrew would lose their lives, seven would be captured and three injured. In London, 216 civilians were killed and another 417 seriously injured.

Then climbing. She is not too good at climbing this time and at 5000m she already begins to vibrate. And even at the target we were no higher than 5200m. There may have been some icing up or some trouble caused by the newly reduced RPM setting. The devil's own Flak over target-heavy, medium and light and rockets. No nightfighter seen. We were once in the searchlights but got out. Fairly considerable searchlight activity. Target marking somewhat late but good. Bombs soon out and away. We saw them explode and hope they took a corner off. Then fuel was short on the return home. Rudi [Uffz Rudolf Budrat] had to pump or we would not have made it. Coming through the snow clouds and snow we probably passed the airfield without seeing it. After firing off reds we came to an airfield – Vitry. A fine large airfield. After landing we went to the HQ and were received by the CO and local Staffelkapitän with cognac. After making out report and drinking a few cognacs we went off by bus to food which was good – broth, roast potatoes, roast meat and red cabbage, lemonade and we went straight to bed and slept well.

Another pilot flying that night was Fw Günther Parge of 4./KG 4 on what was his ninth Frontflug. Even before he joined 4 Staffel, he and his crew almost fell victim to two Typhoons of 174 Sqn flown by Flt Lt Fred Grantham and Flt Sgt George Steel of 174 Sqn when he was attacked on a training flight on 8 January 1944. Since then, his targets had only been London, starting with flying both waves on the first night of *Steinbock*. Of this night he wrote:

It was a bit much on the return flight. According to dead reckoning we were over the Thames estuary. Heavy flak only far right, left and behind us. We went down like a 'piano from the fifth floor' and when we got below the layer of loose clouds, there was no trace of the sea, only beautifully snowy England far and wide. Suddenly a lot of light flak and four-barrelled AA guns, which were supported by 10–15 searchlights. Thank God we were able to disappear again and again in the cloud cover. Cloud coverage approx. 5–7/10th. At Ramsgate we finally reached the coast. Then landing in Brussels instead of Rotterdam after PAN [emergency call] was transmitted and a position received from the air service in Brussels. (The master compass had got jammed and was about 30 degrees incorrect.) Reported to Generalmajor Peltz, a scene which was shown in the 'Deutsche Wochenschau' No.10/44 [German Newsreel] and four photos were published in the *Berliner Illustrierte* [illustrated magazine] on 4 May 1944.

The British assessment was that 92 bombers crossed the coast, of which 25 reached London. Some 606 fires were started in London with another 50 outside, which included Essex, Kent, Suffolk, Surrey and even Wiltshire, while 216 civilians were killed. German analysis was far more optimistic, stating 171 crews had bombed London. Six aircraft failed to return, with another two crashing over France – RAF nightfighters claimed to have destroyed two bombers, probably destroyed one more and damaged one. Eleven Fw 190s of I./SKG 10 then carried out a Störangriff against London between 0335hrs and 0338hrs without loss, but at the same time without any noticeable impact on London. Again, a possible sign of shortages was that Einsatzstaffel IV./KG 101 was flying with KG 54 this night.

The following night saw V./KG 2 and I./SKG 10 being the only protagonists over southeast England. Oblt Helmut Plate of 2./SKG 10 failed to return, while Fw Hermann Bolten and his Bordfunker Fw Wilhelm Lohf were a little luckier. During a nuisance raid on London, he reported he was attacked and badly damaged by a nightfighter. This was probably Flt Sgt Tom Bryan and his Nav/Rad Sgt Basil Friis of 96 Sqn who claimed an Me 410 destroyed – Bolten reported being hit in the port engine and crash-landed at Abbeville at 0317hrs, which matches well with the RAF crew's combat report:

… I attacked from 150yds with two short bursts. Target was then dead ahead and slightly above now flying a fairly steady course, height 17,000ft. There were strikes in the port engine, the e/a took violent evasive action and returned my fire though his aim was wide. I followed him and fired another short burst with no results. E/a now throttled back violently and did a vertical bank to port. I overshot below him and noticed no exhaust flares were visible on the port engine ... I lost my visual as he dived steeply away ...

The night of 22 February 1944 saw yet another attack on London, encouraged by more favourable weather conditions. About 150 bombers began to cross the British coast just after midnight with an unknown number making it to London as well as dropping bombs on nine other counties surrounding the capital. Around 235 fires were started in London and 29 civilians killed. The Germans claimed that 166 out of 185 aircraft made it to London.

Both 2 and 3./KG 100 took part in the attack this night, with RAF Intelligence stating the following, thanks to a talkative prisoner of war:

Flt Lt Reg Pargeter of 29 Sqn, who claimed three aircraft on the night of 24 February 1944. He would shoot down a total of five aircraft, would be awarded the DFC and survived the war having been promoted to Sqn Ldr. (Author's collection)

> KG 100 began to get into its stride as far as timing of attacks was concerned. On this occasion, the Gruppen Kommandeur [Hptm Hans-Gotthelf von Kalckreuth] arrived at Châteaudun and conducted the briefing himself. Time of start was set between 2037 and 2047hrs and the 14 aircraft taking part were lined up at the end of the runway in pre-arranged order. The more experienced crews carried bombloads of two 1800kg and two 1000kg bombs and they were to start first on account of their slower rate of climb. The remainder flew with loads of four 1000kg bombs and started next. All aircraft were to be airborne within the scheduled time and any aircraft delayed more than three minutes beyond its arranged time was not allowed to start. Each aircraft started the take-off run with tail light on and the light was switched off as soon as the aircraft was airborne–a signal that the runway was clear for those following. Aircrafts circled the airfield at a height of 3,000ft in left-hand turns and all set course for the target at pre-arranged times. The coast was crossed at a set time and height which again entailed careful timing.

One He 177A-3 was lost in this attack – Ofw Wolfgang Ruppe's bomber from 3./KG 100 was shot down by Flt Lt Alastair Baillie of 25 Sqn and crashed at Yoxford in Suffolk, killing all but one of the crew. The survivor was the tail gunner, who again was still in the tail when the aircraft hit the ground. RAF nightfighters claimed the destruction of six bombers, probably destroyed one more and damaged one, while RAF intruders claimed to have damaged and destroyed aircraft at Coulommiers in France, destroyed one more at Melsbroek in Belgium and damaged one at Eindhoven in Holland. The Luftwaffe lost eight, with one more crashing in France.

This would see the last night of operations by V./KG 2 as it now became II./KG 51. Two aircraft would still be lost – Uffz Reinhard Eggers of 14./KG 2 was shot down by Sqn Ldr Peter Caldwell of 96 Sqn at Framfield in Sussex, while Lt Felix Müller of 16./KG 2 was plotted approaching High Wycombe in Buckinghamshire from the north only to be engaged by a predicted 3.7in. gun battery. The Me 410's engines were heard to rev up and the aircraft suddenly dived into the ground, killing its crew. Of interest, a document found on the Bordfunker's body gave the Feldpostnummer 52371, which RAF intelligence knew was used by 16./KG 2 and 6./KG 51. In the confusion changing from V./KG 2 to II./KG 51, it would appear that a further Me 410 was lost when Fw Karl Müller and Uffz Kurt Bein, both recorded as being from 16./KG 2 and 6./KG 51, failed to return. Confusion was further compounded with the loss of Lt Felix Müller, but it would appear that Fw Karl Müller was shot down by either Flt Lt Branse Burbridge or Fg Off Edward Hedgecoe of 85 Sqn, who each claimed an Me 410 off Dungeness at roughly the same time.

Twenty-four hours later, the Luftwaffe returned to London. Ogefr Erich Schiml had not taken part in the attack on the night of 22 February as his pilot, Lt Günther Lahl, had toothache and their aircraft, coded 3E+CK, was taken by Uffz Ernst Holst, who returned safely. For 23 February, he wrote:

> Gerd Guder [Uffz Gerhard Guder would move to 2./KG 66 and be killed in action on 18 April 1944] came to me at 0700hrs and asked me to come with him on a test flight. From 0925–0955hrs in the Kommandeur's aircraft 3E+AB. The devil of an aircraft. Back at 1100hrs. Preparations in the afternoon for another sortie. We are not taking part. The Chief [Lt Hans-Friedrich Lenkeit is taking "Caesar" himself. Let's hope it gets back. They rumbled off about 2100hrs … they got back about 0230hrs. All crews back no losses. The Spiess [senior NCO of the Staffel] has just come and told me that our Staffelführer Lt Lenkheit has been shot down over the airfield and our good old "Caesar", our ship of State, is finished. Fw Eder and Uffz Brabant of the crew are in hospital.

Lenkeit flying the Lahl crew's 3E+CK, was shot down near Chièvres by Fg Off Ernest Williams of 605 Sqn, all the crew managing to bale out. Luftwaffe losses this night were light. In addition to Lenkeit, two more aircraft returned with wounded crew, while another suffered engine failure on take-off. Just one aircraft was lost over London, with an unusual ending. Again, the training unit Einsatzstaffel IV./KG 101 was flying this night.

Ju 88A-14 of 6./KG 6. Standing to the left of the gondola is Lt Walter Petrasch, who was killed returning from London on 23 February 1944. (Author's collection)

For the 13 Do 217s of I./KG 2, the target that night was Millwall Docks, which was to be attacked at 4,000m altitude between 2230hrs and 2243hrs, all aircraft but one carrying a single AB1000 and two AB500 incendiary containers. Ofw Hermann Stemann of 2./KG 2 was one of the pilots taking part. He got airborne from Melun-Villaroche in France at 2020hrs, with at least three other aircraft ahead of him, flew towards St-Valery-en-Caux – where he crossed the French coast – and then crossed the English coast at Eastbourne before heading towards London. However, when over the north-west suburbs of the capital, his bomber was picked up by searchlights and then became the target of a highly effective box barrage by anti-aircraft guns. So tremendous was the barrage that it apparently caused panic amongst the crew, who thought their bomber had been hit in the starboard engine, wing and cockpit. Stemann gave the order to bale out and set the Do 217 on autopilot before baling out himself. All four crew were captured none the worse for wear in the Wembley area, but meanwhile the crewless Do 217 continued on its way north-east, losing height gradually.

At Cambridge, Michael J. F. Bowyer, who would become a renowned aviation author and historian after the war, wrote of that night:

> Sirens sounded in Cambridge at 2230hrs and, already recording at my usual vantage point, I noted in my diary two red flares south-south-west, red shell bursts, three large explosions, many incendiary loads south before siren. Just before the All Clear there came an incredibly quiet, low-flying Lancaster going north-east over town. The sound disappeared in the Chesterton direction. I noted it and gave no more thought. By dawn the news spread throughout the town a Dornier had come down last night on allotments close to St George's Church, Chesterton. It had by inches missed the roof of the Chesterton Institution to belly land in the extreme north-east corner of the open ground.

Documentation found in the aircraft gave all the names of those pilots from I./KG 2 flying that night and of those 12 other pilots or aircraft captains. Fw Werner Speiring (3./KG 2) was taken prisoner the following night while Lt Walter Kuttler (3./KG 2) would be killed that same night, Lt Josef Ott (3./KG 2) was killed on 15 March 1944, Uffz Hans Jakob (2./KG 2) was killed on 19 March 1944, Fw Möbius (3./KG 2) was believed killed on 28 June 1944, Lt Hans Böttger (2./KG 2) was killed on 29 June 1944, Ofw Klaus Jäger (3./KG 2) was wounded on 19 April 1944, Lt Roderich von Parpart (3./KG 2) was wounded on 30 July 1944 and Fw Karl Küster (Stab I./KG 2) was killed on 19 August 1944. This was a clear illustration that there was not a very good survival rate for German bomber crews both during *Steinbock* and afterwards over the Normandy beaches.

Between 130 and 160 aircraft flew that night, of which very few made it to London, and yet again bombs were randomly dropped in counties surrounding the capital. In addition to Ernest Williams' claim, Wg Cdr John Cunningham of 85 Sqn was the only other pilot to make a claim that night, a Ju 88 probably destroyed off Beachy Head.

The final major attack against London came on the night of 24 February 1944 – Ogefr Erich Schiml expected to be flying but Lt Lahl's toothache still was no better, so they again stayed behind. The target was government buildings in Westminster by between 135 (British assessment) and 170 (Luftwaffe claims) aircraft. Again, the Luftwaffe failed to achieve a concentration of bombs and again, bombs were spread around London boroughs to the west and southern England. Fw Günther Parge of 4./KG 6 reported that little happened but that having to carry a 'disgusting AB1000 bomb' meant that things were 'stinky and slow', but that their aircraft managed to make it to 6,000m. There was another rise in losses – two Do 217s, two Ju 88s, three Ju 188s and a single He 177 were lost, with a Ju 88 crashing on its return. Twenty-five aircrew were killed and 14 captured. Nightfighter claims were very optimistic with nine destroyed, three probably destroyed and three damaged. Included in these figures were three Me 410s destroyed or probably destroyed – no Me 410s were lost on operations

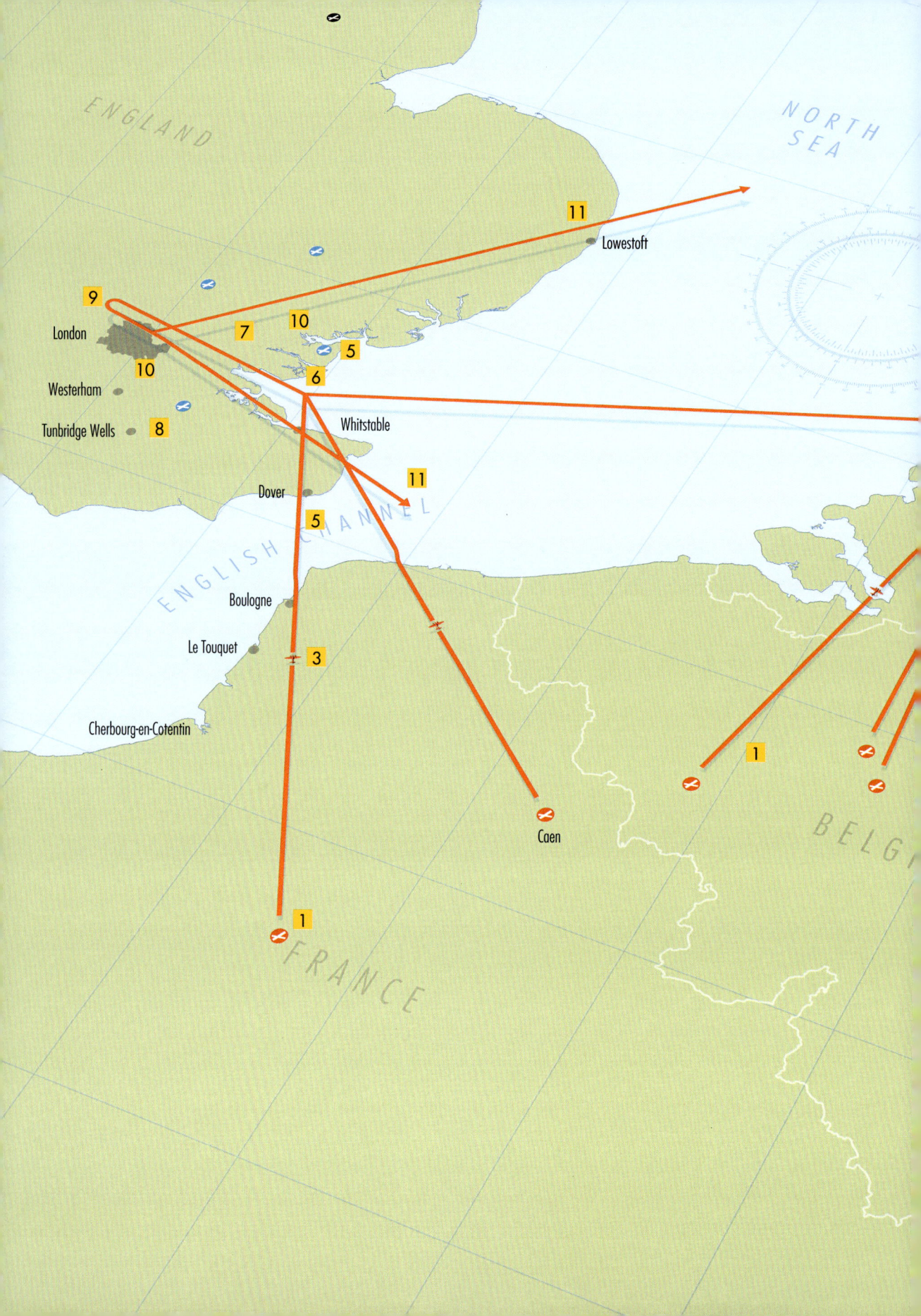

The sixth London raid, Sunday 20 February 1944

This raid was important because it confirmed an impression formed by the British on 18–19 February that the enemy had switched to a new pathfinding and target-marking technique. No longer were attempts made to lay guide lines of incendiaries (*Ablauflinie*) or a sky-marking track (*Leuchtpfad*) to help the main force 'run up' to its target. Instead, I./KG 66 dropped clusters of coloured flares directly over the target, starting several minutes before the first bomber attacked, with frequent renewals of flares to assist later arrivals. These flares acted as aiming points for the bombers, which unloaded their cargoes from a higher altitude, usually without the aid of bomb sights. On 20 February, as described here, the method proved quite effective.

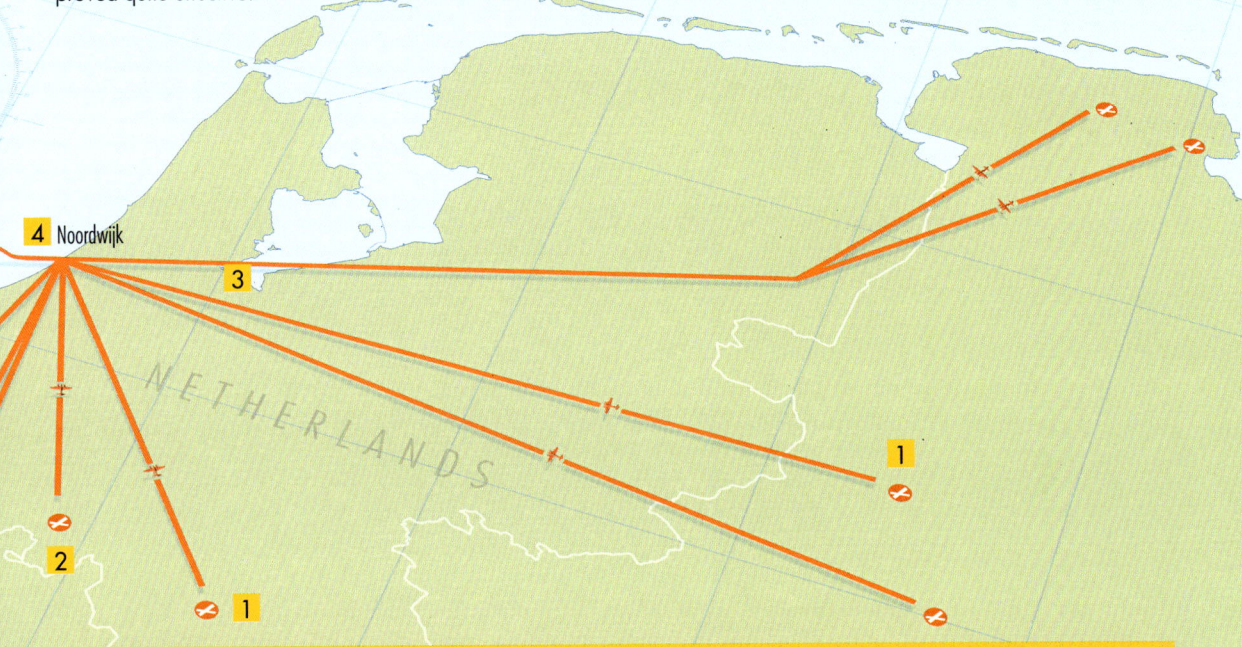

EVENTS

1. 2000–2030hrs. Up to 200 bombers take off from bases in Germany, the Netherlands, Belgium and northern France for the sixth major *Steinbock* raid against London.

2. 2034–2045hrs. Intercepted beam signals, and wireless traffic involving II./KG 6 (operating from Le Culot), provide the British with the first indication of an incoming raid.

3. 2103hrs. ADGB radars identify 30 enemy aircraft (probably from I./KG 66 and II./KG 51) near le Touquet, flying north and north-west, plus 20 planes over Holland, heading west at low altitude.

4. 2110hrs. Main bomber force begins crossing Dutch coast at Noordwijk (M/F beacon No.2 'Nora'), and climbs to reach UK at 16–18,000ft altitude. Extensive use of 'Düppel' from 30 miles off the English coast to target, and also during return, hampers British counter-measures.

5. 2128hrs. First German raider (probably a I./KG 66 pathfinder) makes landfall at Dover. Main force, however, converges over outer Thames estuary, Kent and Essex and continues towards central London, descending to reach attack altitude (in most cases, around 13–16,000ft).

6. 2143hrs. Thames and Medway AA batteries open fire; 5889 x 3.7in. rounds fired by 2235hrs against approaching and departing bombers. One Ju 88 (II./KG 54) shot down into sea off Whitstable at 2155hrs. Some crews drop their bombs over Kent or Essex and flee; others press on towards the target.

7. 2150–2151hrs. German pathfinders begin entering London IAZ. First cascade of white flares over City of London. IAZ batteries open fire.

8. 2155hrs. First target-marker red flares dropped near Royal Tunbridge Wells. Early marking tends to be east or south-east of intended area, probably partly because London is obscured by 10/10ths cloud. Later flares fall further west, as well as on the southern outskirts of Greater London and at Westerham in Kent.

9. 2200–2220hrs. Main attack force arrives. Some planes scatter their bombs across Greater London. Others fly to Brentford area before turning to make their bomb run in a west to east direction, as instructed. Some bomb on red flares and incendiaries already dropped around Kensington, Fulham, Battersea and Wandsworth. Many fires are started in these areas, as well as in Putney and Chiswick as a north-easterly wind blows flares to the south-west, causing bombing to 'drift'. Relatively few bombs fall in the briefed target zone (Walworth – Bermondsey – Camberwell – Peckham area south of the Thames).

10. 2223hrs. London IAZ batteries cease fire as enemy aircraft depart. Between 2151hrs and 2223hrs, IAZ batteries fire 11,415 x 3.7in. and 910 x 5.25in. rounds, plus 348 unguided rockets, against German bombers. One Ju 88 (I./KG 54) is shot down over Croydon at 2210hrs.

11. 2240hrs. Final elements of the German bomber force leave UK air space, mostly via Kent, but in some cases to the north-east, over the Great Yarmouth–Lowestoft area.

A Ju 88S-1 of I./KG 66 being attacked at Montdidier, 30 January 1944. The records of many aircraft damaged or destroyed in 1944 were lost in an air raid before the end of the war. (Author's collection)

Hptm Helmut Fuhrhop, Kommandeur of I./KG 6. He had flown with the Legion Condor but at the start of the war was an instructor. He did not start flying operationally until April 1941, when he was posted to III./KG 51. He then moved to 2./KG 51 and was awarded the Ritterkreuz in November 1943, having flown over 200 missions. After a short period as a staff officer, he was posted to KG 6 and took command of I./KG 6 in April 1943. He would be killed in action on 29 February 1944. (Author's collection)

(V./KG 2 now being II./KG 51) for over another month. 29 Sqn was particularly active, with Fg Off John Barry claiming two, and Flt Lt Reg Pargeter and Fg Off Bill Provan three each.

The remainder of February 1944 was a non-event in respect of Luftwaffe attacks, albeit on 25 February 1944, an He 177 of 3./KG 100 was shot down by 331 Sqn near St Trond while on a training flight, and a Ju 188 of 4./KG 2 was shot down on transfer flight from Coulommiers to Münster, probably by 379th Fighter Sqn. It was becoming clear that the threat of flying unescorted bombers in daylight from one airfield to another was risky, and that is most graphically illustrated by what happened to Maj Helmut Fuhrhop, Kommandeur of I./KG 6, on 29 February 1944. Ogefr Erich Schiml explains the background:

Wake up at 0900hrs. Off at 0910hrs. Moving. Take off at 1020hrs and land at 1110hrs at Dreux. Then lunch. It was the devil's own hedge-hopping with Ofw Springer and Uffz Weisselstein. Rest in the afternoon. Shave and wash. The evening meal at 1700hrs. A balloon is said to be going up. It cannot be bad if it is against some other dung heap and not London. Briefing by the Pippin who told us of the loss of the Kommandeur and Uffz Meyer. Attack on Plymouth. As he is giving us landing and take-off instructions a telephone call comes through from Bohnau [Oblt Harald Bohnau] "Operation called off!".

Early in the afternoon of 29 February 1944, Maj Helmut Fuhrhop took off from Chièvres together with another Ju 188 flown by Uffz Wilhelm Mayer of 1./KG 6. Each aircraft carried a crew of five as well as passengers and was headed for Dreux in preparation for missions later that day. In Meyer's aircraft was a groundcrew man and Oblt Rolf Hailbronner, the highly experienced Gruppe Technical Officer, as veteran of the Legion Condor and holder of the Deutsches Kreuz in Gold and

Typhoons of 609 Sqn taxiing out for a mission over France. 609 Sqn, which was commanded by Sqn Ldr Johnnie Wells and based at RAF Manston in Kent, was responsible for the death of Maj Helmut Fuhrhop of I./KG 6 on 29 February 1944. (Author's collection)

Ehrenpokal, while Helmut's aircraft carried a single groundcrew man and Helmut's two dogs – Chica and Ciro.

At 1120hrs, nine Hawker Typhoons of 609 Sqn lifted off from RAF Manston in Kent and with two other squadrons, were tasked to carry out fighter sweeps in support of Ramrod 603. 609's route took them to Domburg–Florennes–Le Culot–Cambrai in France, during which time two pilots were separated and forced to attack targets by themselves (and during one attack, one of the Typhoons was shot down by Flak and the pilot killed). The remaining pilots, led by Sqn Ldr Johnny Wells, carried on, attacking barges and tugs, before spotting two Ju 188s flying south-west at about 1,000ft west of Cambrai. The combat report detailing what happened next no longer exists, but one Belgian pilot flying that day, Fg Off Charles De Moulin, wrote of it in his biography:

> Suddenly, two shadows cross our path, just above us, and then disappear to our left into broken cloud. Not fast enough to prevent me from identifying two fat, juicy Ju 188s. The three of us [Flt Lt Lawrence Smith & Fg Off Georges Jaspis were the other two pilots], at great risk of collision, make a sharp turn without waiting for the other Typhoons to join in the chase. It is a free for all. Full throttle, screaming engine and fingers on the gun button, we go flat out after the Ju 188s and within a few seconds come across them in a clear patch of sky … In front of me, multi-coloured ribbons stream towards my Typhoon and I can see the gunner of the second bomber throwing tracer at me. A little rudder to correct and his turret becomes mute as the gunner crumples on his seat …

The combat was a slaughter, with all seven Typhoons joining in, each of the seven pilots being credited with the kills. With both bombers a ball of flame, Meyer's bomber crashed at Bohain-en-Vermandois and Helmut's bomber at Seboncourt, 5km south of Meyer's crash site. There were no survivors. Apparently, Charles De Moulin's Typhoon was damaged when one of the Ju 188s exploded, but he makes no mention of this in his memoirs. Fuhrhop together with his two dogs and all the others killed that day were buried with full military honours at Mons on 5 March 1944; his place as Gruppen Kommandeur was taken by Ritterkreuz winner Hptm Hans Thurner, Staffelkapitän of 6./KG 6.

It was becoming clear that with such continued heavy losses across all Geschwader, the intensity of *Steinbock* attacks would now start to wane and the Luftwaffe for the next three

The funeral of all of the I./KG 6 aircrew and groundcrew killed by 609 Sqn on 29 February 1944. Seen in the front row 4th from right are Oberst Hermann Hogeback (Kommodore KG 6), Maj Rudolf Puchinger (Kdr III./KG 6, 3rd from right) and Maj Johann Thurner (Kdr I./KG 6, 2nd from right). (Author's collection)

months could do little apart from preparing for the inevitable Allied invasion with a much-depleted bomber force. For example, the Do 217, which was now being operated by only I and III./KG 2, had very few aircraft available and this was not helped by I./KG 2 starting to convert to the Ju 188 at the end of March 1944. Strangely, the Luftwaffe thought the month had gone well, writing: 'To sum up: by exploiting previously gained experience, the Luftwaffe was during February 1944 able to achieve results very satisfactory in proportion to our strength of effort.'

This would all change in March 1944.

Loading an AB1000 container to a Ju 88A of I./KG 76, Varrelbusch, early 1944. The container could hold 620 10kg incendiary bombs. (Author's collection)

Starting to change – March 1944

March 1944 would see *Steinbock* targets starting to change but not immediately, as Ogefr Erich Schiml wrote, somewhat tongue in cheek, for the attack on the night of 1 March:

> Off at 2240hrs. Briefing at 2300hrs. "New target"–beginning with L! We again, as the only ones with four 500SC and 50 BC last to take off with the tired 3E+GK. We try to start–1 … 2 … 10–nothing. Hell! The dog just will not come. One engine starts up, there is not a sound from the other. In the end, the others have all gone–10 of them–and we are still there. At last we taxi to the take off–get a red in front and stay put. We are not allowed off. It might have been done but Tommy is already flying over us so we miss another good sortie.

Lt Wilhelm Werner, 2./KG 100, whose He 177 was shot down by Wg Cdr Bob Braham (flying with 613 Sqn), 5 March 1944. The sight of the exhaust plumes as Werner was about to take off attracted Braham to what would be another victory for this successful pilot. (Author's collection)

British sources believed that 70 aircraft crossed the coast but very few made it to London. German sources state that 131 out of 164 crews made it to London but that does not explain why the bombing, yet again, was spread across the Home Counties. Thirty-four civilians were killed, with 18 of the fatalities occurring when a bomb landed on a terraced row of houses in and around Station Road, Strood in Kent – the youngest to lose their life was five, the oldest 75.

German losses were light – a Ju 88A of 2./KG 54 and an He 177 of 2./KG 100 were the only losses over or off the UK – but one bomber crashed on take-off, four crashed on their return, while a Ju 88S-1 of Einsatz Staffel I./KG 66 flown by Ofw Rolf Stoop was shot down by a nightfighter and crashed near St Omer, possibly the Me 410 claimed by Fg Off Bill Gough of 96 Sqn near Boulogne. RAF claims were again optimistic, with five German bombers destroyed and one damaged.

For almost the next two weeks, the Luftwaffe was a rare sight over the United Kingdom. Fw Günther Parge of 4./KG 6 flew on 1 March and then not again until 14 March 1944. Ogefr Erich Schiml indicated in his diary that on 2 March 1944, they were to attack an unspecified coastal target, not London – which was greeted with enthusiasm until it was cancelled. The next mission was 13 March – London again – but that too was scrubbed. For much of the two weeks, all they did was say goodbye to a number of crews posted to I./KG 66 on 3 March, bury the crews killed on 29 February and on 5 March, and sleep, eat and drink for the rest of the time.

Very few losses occurred during this time, but one of note occurred on the afternoon of 5 March 1944. Lt Wilhelm Werzer was an experienced pilot with 3./KG 100, having flown with 1 and 4./KG 4 over the Eastern Front since July 1942 and being awarded the Frontflugspange in Gold in January 1943 and the Ehrenpokal in October 1943, by which time he had been commissioned as a Leutnant in July 1943. After the war, his wife Elfriede found out what had happened:

> On 5 March 1944, a sunny Sunday, my then 29 year-old husband was to undertake a short routine test flight from Châteaudun to test a repaired wing. At the last moment, two crew members were changed and as a result, the plane stood still on the runway for several minutes. A tall cloud of dust and exhaust fumes swept into the sky, visible far into the countryside. The British fighter saw the cloud. The pilot was one of the most decorated nightfighters, Wg Cdr Bob Braham. Unbelievably daring, he flew over several German Flak positions towards the airfield. The soldiers on the ground took him for a returning fighter of their own and waved at him. Not to cause any suspicion, Braham returned their wave. When he saw that my husband had no fighter protection, he shot him down 300m above the airstrip. The bomber rolled onto its back and crashed. I assume that my husband was killed by machine gun fire and knew nothing.

The scene at Eastbourne railway station on 14 March 1944 following a visit by Fw 190s of I./SKG 10 the previous night. (Author's collection)

All five crew were killed when the He 177 crashed on the airfield. Werzer had flown 127 operational flights over Russia plus another four with 3./KG 100 during *Steinbock*. He was again the type of experienced bomber pilot the Luftwaffe could ill afford to lose.

The Luftwaffe was back for its first major attack of March 1944 on the night of the 14th. Ogefr Erich Schiml, who was not to know he would be dead in eight days' time, wrote about the attack in some detail, excited to be on operations again for the first time since 20 February 1944:

> Rest ordered for today, it looks as if something were happening again. 1715hrs dinner leave for briefing at 1830hrs. At last it has worked. Take off 60 minutes late at 2115hrs for the first time with 3E+MK. She is not too bad. The engines good. Then came the crazy approach. First out to sea on a line Norwich to Rotterdam; from there towards Cambridge then turning point to London. From there to Calais, Le Havre and home. Bomb load two AB1000 and 10 x Br.C.50. Approach height 6500m over target 5000m. One nightfighter between Cambridge and London. Amazing powerful searchlights and ground marking for nightfighters in the northern area of the approach i.e. Cambridge-Ipswich-Norwich. Colossal rocket Flak over the target. Some heavy Flak on the return flight at the coast more rockets and searchlights....On coming through the clouds, we see an airfield and land in spite of failure of the approach lighting and artificial horizon. We taxi to the lights and see that we are at Abbeville half an hour from our own airfield. Two Ju 88s of KG 30 from Germany arrive and a Do 217 makes a crash-landing.

The Luftwaffe believed that the attacking force of around 140 managed to reach London but the effects were not worth the effort. Furthermore, nightfighters and intruders were active, claiming ten bombers destroyed and one probably destroyed. The losses suffered by the attackers were severe, with nine lost over the United Kingdom or failing to return, one being shot down by an intruder on its return and two crashing on their return. In addition to this, I./KG 51, which had recently joined the battle, suffered an Me 410 crashing on take-off from St André, killing Deutsches Kreuz winner Oblt Werner Pape, while a second 410

Air Marshal Sir Roderic Hill (AOC ADGB, 3rd from right) visiting the crash site of the Ju 88A-4 of 4./KG 30 flown by Lt Eginhardt Wolf, 22 March 1944, with crews from 488 Sqn. Left to right: Flt Lt C. P. Reed (Nav/Rad), Sqn Ldr Nigel Bunting, Flt Lt John Hall, Air Marshal Hill, Wg Cdr Dick Haine (OC 488 Sqn) and Flt Sgt J. L. Wood. (Author's collection)

crashed in flames near Beauvais returning from the attack, also killing both crew. I./SKG 10 is also believed to have lost three Fw 190s, possibly on a failed diversionary sortie to Plymouth. The human cost that night was 47 killed and nine captured. Three of those captured were from 8./KG 6 who, with a Ju 88 on fire and lost, baled out, leaving the pilot to be killed in the crash near Devizes in Wiltshire, some 90 miles from central London; while Uffz Josef Wiesmaier of 4./KG 30 found himself in mid-air when the gondola of his Ju 88 in which he was lying was shot away, throwing him into the night sky. His pilot, Lt Eginhart Wolf, returned with two crew only for them to be shot down on 22 March 1944; this time Wolf and two crew, which included Wiesmaier's replacement Uffz Theo Rakowski, were killed and one captured. Of the attack, the Luftwaffe rather more truthfully wrote:

> During the attack on London on the night of 14–15 March, carried out by 187 aircraft, weather conditions necessitated a last minute postponement by one hour of the time of the attack and the absence from operations of I./KG 100, I./SKG 10 and about half the aircraft of I./KG 51. Target marking was carried out five minutes after H-hour and was not subsequently renewed so that it quickly disappeared in the clouds. We did not succeed in concentrating our attack in the target area.

If this night was not bad, things would continue the following day. Ogefr Erich Schiml wrote that they had a good breakfast at Abbeville and despite minor Flak damage to the fuselage and propeller, expected to take off for Chièvres at 0800hrs only for the starboard engine not to start. Despite a warning that enemy aircraft were around, they took off 30 minutes later, landing without incident. However, after they left the airfield, it was attacked by 35 B-26s of the 322nd and four from the 323rd Bomb Group, 9th Air Force. The workshops were badly damaged and two aircraft destroyed – 3E+RK and their Flak-damaged 3E+MK.

The days that followed were much quieter, with just Störangriff against London by Me 410s and Fw 190s over the next two nights, their results being described by the British as 'trivial'. After I./KG 6 moved to Melsbroek on 18 March 1944, the attack that night was cancelled.

Of interest, nine crews from II./KG 6 flew to Wien-Aspern in Austria that same day to carry out a daylight bombing mission in support of ground troops in the Budapest area, returning to Le Culot on 21 March.

At long last, on 19 March 1944, the target changed from London to Hull, but yet again, the results of the bombing could be described as trivial; the losses were another matter. Of the 131 bombers the Luftwaffe claimed to attack, the RAF claimed just 90 made it over the coast and, 'The enemy claims to have attacked Hull. No bombs fell on Hull and negligible harm was done by air activity.' There were no reports of civilian deaths that night. However, nine aircraft failed to return, which meant 38 aircrew were killed and just one captured. Amongst those killed were Hptm Walter Schmitt, Staffelkapitän of 2./KG 66 (shot down by Flt Lt Joe Singleton of 25 Sqn), and Hptm Heinrich Müller of 2./KG 100 (shot down by Plt Off Jan Brochocki of 307 Sqn). Schmitt, former Staffelkapitän of 5./KG 6, would be awarded the Deutsches Kreuz in Gold posthumously. His loss had a direct impact on the failure of the attack that night. Singleton, whose son Peter would coincidentally be the author's Flt Commander at RAF Cranwell in 1980, did not realise the significance of his victory:

> Identified as Ju 188 (by pilot and Nav/Rad) and closed to about 100yds and gave a 2½ second burst at 100yds from dead astern. Strikes were scored on fuselage immediately followed by a big explosion. As we were still closing we saw German markings on the tail and had to pull up steeply to avoid collision; debris from the e/a spattered our aircraft. We orbited and watched e/a go down in a steep dive to port in flames. When the e/a had dropped about 5,000ft it broke up completely and several burning pieces were seen to hit the sea, casting a glow over a wide area.

Maj Hermann Schmidt, Kdr I./KG 66, following the award of his Ritterkreuz, 20 April 1944. He received this award in person from Oberst Peltz. (Author's collection)

Schmitt's Ju 88S hit the sea 55 miles north-north-east of Cromer at 2120hrs. Singleton and his Nav/Rad Fg Off Bill Haslam then claimed a second Ju 188 seven minutes later 65 miles north-north-east of Cromer, and a third five minutes after that 80 miles north-north-east of Cromer. However, during the course of this combat, both glycol tanks were hit by debris from the doomed German aircraft. With the port engine spewing sparks and the starboard overheating, Joe decided to land with the wheels and flaps up, but then the starboard engine burst into flames:

> I switched on the port landing light since a crash looked inevitable and I was hoping it would help; unfortunately it was not fully down when we landed. I tried to get more power out of the port engine which however seized. We got down into the red of the angle of glide then the red disappeared and I levelled out a bit and suddenly felt the aircraft hit the ground. Nav/Rad opened the top hatch and jumped out, I followed a few seconds later and we got about 25yds away from aircraft. We sat down and after about half a minute I saw that both engines were burning at the cylinder heads. I went back and climbed into the cockpit switching off all the switches and looked for the fire extinguisher. I was unable to find it so gathered handfuls of soil and threw them onto the engines. As most of the starboard engine cowling had been burnt away I was able to put the soil right on the fire; this seemed effective and the flames went out. We walked to the nearest road and were picked up by the ambulance.

Joe's claim for a Ju 188 at 2120hrs was the first that night. He was the only pilot to claim a Ju 188 or 88 that night and the only losses were three Ju 88s from 5./KG 30 flown by Ofw Werner Weil, Fw Fritz Stenutz and Uffz Ulrich Gerlach, another from 6./KG 30 flown by Fw Rudolf Junger and one from 1./KG 54 flown by Lt Ferdinand Stadtmüller; all failed to return and must have come down in the North Sea.

Ogefr Erich Schiml wrote that he was quite excited that, at last, London was not the target on this night:

> At last all the luggage comes but I shall not unpack much. There's an operation in the evening. 1800hrs briefing. Drove there in a bus. 13 crews and all the Staffelkapitän. Today we go to Hull. Nora-sea turning point-Hull. Take off at 1948hrs. Attack between 2200hrs and 2212hrs. Approach low-level over Holland and then quite low over the sea to the climbing point. Climbing then with 1.2 boost over the turning point (well marked but too far to the left) about 4000m. Knickebein was further to the right. In this way we got to the coast too early, south of Hull somewhat north of The Wash. Here we stooged around, searched for by a thousand searchlights using up valuable fuel until 10 minutes after Zero Hour the lighting was laid over Hull. We see it far away to the right and fly off for the bombing run. We were the last to drop our load into the town which was burning at every corner. Out of 2900ltr of fuel, we have now only 800ltr left and must make for home. Direct to Nora. Arrived at Nora and through flying at most economical speed still had 500–600ltr. Made a good landing at home at 2347hrs.

Hptm Helmut Heisig, Staffelkapitän 1./SKG 10, shot down by Sqn Ldr Bernard Thwaites of 85 Sqn, 24 March 1944. An experienced He 111 pilot on the Eastern Front, Heisig did not last long on the Western Front. (Author's collection)

This being the first *Steinbock* attack away from London, it was a total failure despite what crews and the Luftwaffe thought – RAF nightfighters claiming eight bombers destroyed. To now lose more trained crews on what in hindsight was a waste of effort could not be sustained and the true effectiveness of *Steinbock* was becoming futile. However, worse would follow. Following the problems attacking London on 14 March, of the Hull attack, the Luftwaffe wrote:

> Similar difficulties were experienced during the attack by 131 aircraft on 19/20 March on Hull when the loss of the first pathfinder aircraft led to target marking being five minutes late. Further navigational troubles resulted in a wide dispersal of attack. The most optimistic estimate would be that half the bombs fell in the target area.

Optimistic indeed! Nothing occurred the following night, allowing Erich Schiml to sleep, eat and pack; on 21 March 1944, he wrote:

> Slept until 0900hrs then loaded up packed hand luggage and bedding for possible operation. Prepare for another night in the monastery in Zawernden [believed to be Monastery of the Visitation, Zaventem]. The others go by train. We are to go to Couvron by aircraft after one more sortie (our sixth).

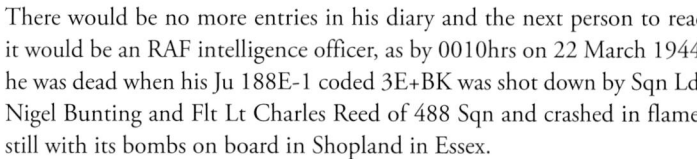

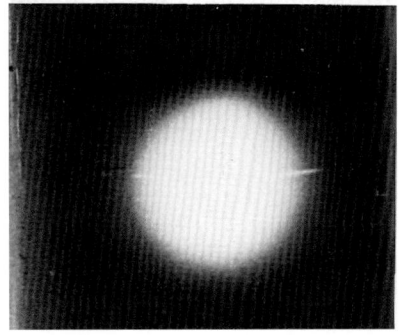

The end of Lt Wolfgang Krahner's Fw 190G-2 of I./SKG 10, 22 March 1944. (Author's collection)

Flt Lt Norman Head of 96 Sqn (seen here in a Beaufighter when he was with 409 Sqn). He would shoot down four aircraft between 2 January and 22 March 1944, with two probably destroyed on 21 January 1944. (Author's collection)

There would be no more entries in his diary and the next person to read it would be an RAF intelligence officer, as by 0010hrs on 22 March 1944, he was dead when his Ju 188E-1 coded 3E+BK was shot down by Sqn Ldr Nigel Bunting and Flt Lt Charles Reed of 488 Sqn and crashed in flames still with its bombs on board in Shopland in Essex.

The night of 21 March 1944 saw a return to London with around 140 aircraft, of which 95 were stated as crossing the coast. With the main target stated as being Westminster Abbey, again bombs were scattered across London and the Home Counties. 237 fires were reported in London, with around 39 civilians killed and 225 seriously injured. Nightfighters were successful yet again, claiming eight destroyed and five damaged. Flt Lt Johnnie Surman and his Nav/Rad Flt Sgt Clarence Weston claimed 604 Sqn's first kills, having converted from Beaufighters to the Mosquito Mk XIII, shooting down the Ju 88A-4 flown by Lt Eginhart Wolf of 4./KG 30 at Latchingdon in Essex; they were detached to 410 Sqn that night to gain operational experience with the new type, flying from RAF Castle Camps in Cambridgeshire. In total, eight German aircraft were lost and two crashed on their return.

There was an unusual success for one of the German bombers, albeit pyrrhic. Shot down by Flt Lt John Hall of 488 Sqn, the Ju 88A-14 of 8./KG 6 flown by Oblt Hans Diblik crashed onto the airfield at Earls Colne in Essex. The explosion, as it still had three crew and its bombs on board, destroyed a parked Marauder bomber, serial 41-31627 codenamed YA-Q and named 'Perkatory' of the 555th Bomb Sqn, 386th Bomb Group.

The next two nights saw yet more Störangriff by nine Fw 190s and ten Me 410s on the night of 22 March, and seven Fw 190s and nine Me 410s on the night after. Their bombs had minimal effect but Flt Lt Norman Head of 96 Sqn accounted for Lt Wolfgang Krahner of Stab I./SKG 10 off Pevensey at 2120hrs on 22 March 1944:

After some minutes contact was obtained on e/a at three miles range and below crossing from port to starboard at height of approximately 23,000ft. Mosquito turned in behind and closed to 1½ miles and then used Nitrous Oxide for one minute. This gave sufficient extra speed to enable Mosquito to close in on the target which was taking medium evasive action and travelling on an approximate course of 350 degrees. At 700ft range a visual of an Fw 190 was obtained and Flt Lt Head gave a short burst from 300ft and saw the e/a explode and disintegrate with pieces of burning wreckage flying off. On landing pieces of wreckage were found in the port engine air intake of the Mosquito.'

If that was not bad enough for I./SKG 10, Sqn Ldr Bernard Thwaites of 85 Sqn then accounted for Hptm Helmut Heisig, Staffelkapitän of 1./SKG 10, at 0012hrs on 24 March 1944, the Fw 190 catching fire in the engine and fuselage, and going down in flames and crashing into the sea off the French coast between Boulogne and Berck-sur-Mer. Heisig was another highly experienced bomber pilot who had received the Deutsches Kreuz in Gold flying with 2./KG 4 in January 1943.

Again, positioning from one airfield to another in preparation for an attack was still fraught with danger in more ways than one, and on 23 March 1944, almost resulted in the loss of another future Ritterkreuzträger. Flt Lt Barry Needham and Fg Off Don Laubman of 412 Sqn were in one of a number of Spitfires of 126 Wg escorting

72 Marauders attacking Creil Marshalling Yard. At 1200hrs, they spotted an aircraft low at three o'clock. Barry Needham asked to investigate and dived from 14,000ft to tree height, identifying the aircraft as a Ju 88. At 1110hrs, Maj Hermann Schmidt, Kommandeur of I./KG 66, had got airborne from Avord to pre-position for an attack that night. Schmidt was a highly experienced pathfinder pilot who had flown with KGr 100 from the start of the war, and in April 1943, took command of the newly formed I./KG 66. At 1150hrs, his crew spotted the two approaching fighters, thinking they were Mustangs. Barry Needham relates what happened next:

> At about 100yds from about five degrees starboard I gave it a short burst and the port engine burst into flames. I overshot and throttled back until I was again behind the 88. I gave him another short burst from port observing strikes on the port engine and wing. The 88 then turned into a large field and landed wheels up. Four men were seen to get out and I called the Wg Cdr Flying for permission to shoot them on the ground. This was granted and I saw the four men double up on the ground.

Schmidt crash-landed near Senlis at 1150hrs, and he and Uffz Heinz Knode were apparently unharmed (albeit they did not fly again until 12 April 1944). Bordfunker Ofw Eduard Zech was killed and groundcrew Uffz Friedrich Grove was wounded. Schmidt, who had already been awarded the Ehrenpokal and Deutsches Kreuz in Gold, would receive the Ritterkreuz on 20 April 1944.

24 March 1944 started badly for 2./KG 6. Lt Hans-Friedrich Lenkeit, Staffelführer of 2./KG 6, was again shot down, this time by German Flak while on a positioning flight; he had only recently recovered from being shot down by an intruder on 24 February 1944; this time, his injuries meant that he did not return to take command of training unit 11./KG 6 until the summer, but did survive the war. It is believed his place was taken by Hptm Erwin Lissat, who would be killed on 28 May 1944.

The night of 24 March 1944 saw a concentrated attack by around 140 crews against London, with aircraft crossing the coast between Portsmouth to the west and Southwold to the east, with the main effort concentrated on 'government buildings' in Whitehall; again, the bombs came down on 23 London boroughs, most of them south of the Thames. Thirty-nine civilians lost their lives, with another 118 seriously injured. Fw Günther Parge of 4./KG 6 had recently returned from Austria and had cause to remember this attack very well:

> This was our wildest sortie. "Lucie" (3E+LM) was "angry" because our good Number 1 ground mechanic Willi Weiss had not refilled the coolant and we had to fly with open radiator flaps.
>
> Over the English coast, at a height of 4800m, we dropped five 50kg bombs on the searchlights. However, in the course of the manoeuvres, we reach a height of 5500m but still lag behind the main force.

Flt Lt Barry Needham of 412 Sqn, who together with Fg Off Don Laubman shot down the Ju 188 flown by Maj Hermann Schmidt, Kommandeur of I./KG 66, 23 March 1944. Schmidt, who was a highly experienced pathfinder, was lucky to have survived. (Author's collection)

Fg Off Tom Condon and Wg Cdr Keith Hampshire, Commanding Officer of 456 Sqn, visit the remains of Hptm Anton Oeben's Ju 88A-4 of 6./KG 6, Walberton, West Sussex, 25 March 1944. (Author's collection)

On the way to the target, wild evasive actions begin – out of the searchlights and back in again. But they are not able to keep us in their searchlight cones.

An extensive fire at the target, bombs have been dropped over the entire target area. In order not to drop the bombs where there is already a fire, we drop them south of the large bend of the river Thames – a compensation for [the bombing of] Dithmarscherstraße 16 (by the way, the constant tone from 'Elektra', which is – strangely enough – not disturbed [Elektra Sonne-radio navigation system]).

Now return flight course north. We are taken into the loving arms of the searchlights. We fight for our lives but are not able to reach the coast, because the Flak always forces us west. But I have to get through this.

Physically I am completely finished and I shout: "Helmut [Fw Helmut Dyderski, Beobachter], I can't go on any longer. When do we reach the coast?" With the whole weight of my body, I continue flying evasive manoeuvres. At long last there is a barely recognizable light strip of land the coast!

The aircraft trimmed nose heavy and diving like mad, we soon roar over the sea. The FuG 101 [radio altimeter] signal drops down just a few meters above zero. By hair's breadth we miss colliding with a fishing vessel that is travelling without lights.

Then, over the sea, we can no longer find the Lux buoys and turn by dead reckoning. As intended, an illuminated airfield can be seen near our own coast. Of course we think it would be Vlissingen (on course), but it might have been Ostende, because we do not find our airfield. After we have flown for about 15 minutes, there are clouds at 500m and far away a bright light. We fly there and drop through the clouds very carefully. Fuel only for 20 minutes. We turn around and fly west. After 10 minutes the cloud cover breaks up and down there is an airfield, we land at Metz – four men hug each other.

It was another night which saw heavy Luftwaffe casualties – ten aircraft failed to return while another seven either crashed on take-off or on the return. Another 46 aircrew lost their lives, with just five being captured. *Steinbock* was bleeding the Luftwaffe's bomber force dry and worse was to come before March 1944 was out. The Luftwaffe thought the attack had been a success but wrote that 'heavy losses were sustained'.

The night of 27 March 1944 saw the last major attack of the month and the second against a target away from London. Bristol, a port on the Severn Estuary, was being used for the build-up for the invasion of France; the Home Security wrote the following concerning the attack:

> A force of about 112 aircraft operated overland for about two hours. The majority crossed the coast between Plymouth and Weymouth and scattered over an area bounded by Lands End/Cardiff/Banbury/Reading/Selsey Bill; the remainder made shallow penetrations over south-eastern England. So widespread and ineffectual were these operations that it is difficult to tell from the bombing what the target was. The enemy claims Bristol and also London although in fact no bombs fell on either.

German propaganda made quite a bit of this attack, which was analysed afterwards by the British who, in their analysis, began by saying:

> While the pattern of German propaganda descriptions of raids on Great Britain remains constant, in no previous instance has distortion reached so fine a point as in accounts of attacks on Bristol which, it was claimed, the Luftwaffe had undertaken during the night of 27–28 March …
>
> Their preposterous claims are the more interesting when contrasted with the Home Security analysis …

Lt Ernst-Karl Fara of 2./KG 66 visiting the remains of his Ju 188E-1. Damaged by Flak over Bristol on the night of 27 March 1944, he and his crew successfully baled out near Dieppe. He is holding a piece of the fuselage skin, which shows part of the aircraft's code Z6+AK. (Author's collection)

Ten aircraft failed to return while three crashed on their return. Again, the human cost was high – 29 were killed and unusually, 19 were taken prisoner, their subsequent interrogations being of great value to the RAF. The attack on London was as a result of an ineffective *Störangriff* by ten Fw 190s of I./SKG 10. Flt Lt Ken Kennedy of 96 Sqn claimed the destruction of one of these fighter-bombers off Dungeness just before midnight but none were reported lost.

Fw Günther Parge of 4./KG 6 also took part in the attack on Bristol, flying from Dreux in France and landing back there at 0148hrs. This was unfortunate as he noted that later that day, his beloved 3E+LM was destroyed by fighters – Spitfires of 441 Sqn led by Wg Cdr 'Hawkeye' Wells strafed the airfield, claiming to have damaged and destroyed a number of German aircraft – another example of why it was becoming harder to ensure that *Steinbock* was remaining effective. Not only was the Luftwaffe losing substantial numbers during the attacks, but they were now increasingly falling victim to Allied aircraft over the Continent.

Of this last attack of the month, the Luftwaffe thought it had been successful 'despite heavy enemy defences, including single-engined fighters and rocket Flak fire'. It could not have been much further from the truth.

Failure at Bristol, 27–28 March 1944

This operation was notable for two things. The first was its appalling inaccuracy – until German propaganda claimed that heavy damage had been inflicted on Bristol, the British wondered if the city was even a target. Secondly, the raid produced a large haul of prisoners – 19 airmen, which was more than in any UK raid since mid-1941, and 14.5% of all prisoners taken during *Steinbock*. As such, the raid represented a valuable intelligence coup, as well as an obvious military failure for Peltz's forces.

EVENTS

1. 2125–2140hrs. I. and II./KG 54 take off from forward operating bases in north-eastern France. Their target is Bristol docks, to arrive between 0000hrs and 0006hrs. They are joined by KG 30 and KG 6 bombers temporarily based near Paris, and by KG 2, operating from Vannes and Nantes. Their intended route is via Guernsey across Lyme Bay and south-west England to the mouth of the River Usk, then east to Chepstow before carrying out a north-south bomb run across Bristol and starting their return journey to France.

2. 2310–2320hrs. German bombers converge on Guernsey, flying at 13–14,500ft. For navigation purposes, Guernsey is marked by a cone of six searchlights. The force continues northwards, dropping 'Düppel' as it approaches the British coast.

3. 2300hrs onwards. The British know an attack is likely. Warnings to Kriegsmarine authorities that aircraft will operate over the western part of the Channel have been intercepted, and medium-frequency signals between bombers and their ground control stations are monitored from soon after take-off. As the German force heads north, it is tracked by British radar. The RAF's 80 Wing implements electronic counter-measures, AA batteries are placed on high alert and nightfighters are scrambled from bases across the southern half of the UK. Smoke screens are ignited at Plymouth, Cardiff and Newport, while decoy sites are also put into operation outside Bristol and Weston-super-Mare.

4. 2325–2340hrs. I./KG 66 aircraft make landfall between Plymouth and Weymouth. HAA batteries around the Isle of Portland, Exeter and Plymouth open fire. Evidence suggests serious navigational errors among the pathfinders, with over fifty flares dropped by 2345hrs around Weymouth, Plymouth and other locations far from the target or intended turning points. Numerous flares continue to be dropped over land and sea near Weymouth throughout the operation, for no obvious reason.

5. 2335–2345hrs. Main bomber force arrives over the UK, scattered across a broad front between Land's End and the Isle of Wight. Individual aircraft wander as far east as the London IAZ, as far west as Carmarthenshire, and as far north as Shropshire. Bombs are dumped over a wide area, causing minimal damage and few casualties.

6. 2345–0015hrs. Some bombers manage to stay on approximately the correct course towards turning points along the south Wales coast. Several are shot down by nightfighters or AA fire before they can locate their target. From 2359–0015hrs, some concentrations of marker flares are achieved in the Cardiff – Newport – Chepstow – Avonmouth – Weston-super-Mare area. These attract a mixture of HE and incendiary bombs, as does a decoy site near Weston. But not a single flare or bomb falls within Bristol, or even close to the city.

7. 0015hrs onwards. Most of the attack force begins its return to France. A few planes continue to circle over the south-west in a fruitless search for their target. Flares are reported at Weston as late as 0100hrs and a bomber is shot down south of Bristol at the same time.

8. 0118hrs. The UK is clear of raiders. ADGB makes its final claim of the operation, when a nightfighter crew reports shooting a bomber into the sea 50 miles south of Brighton.

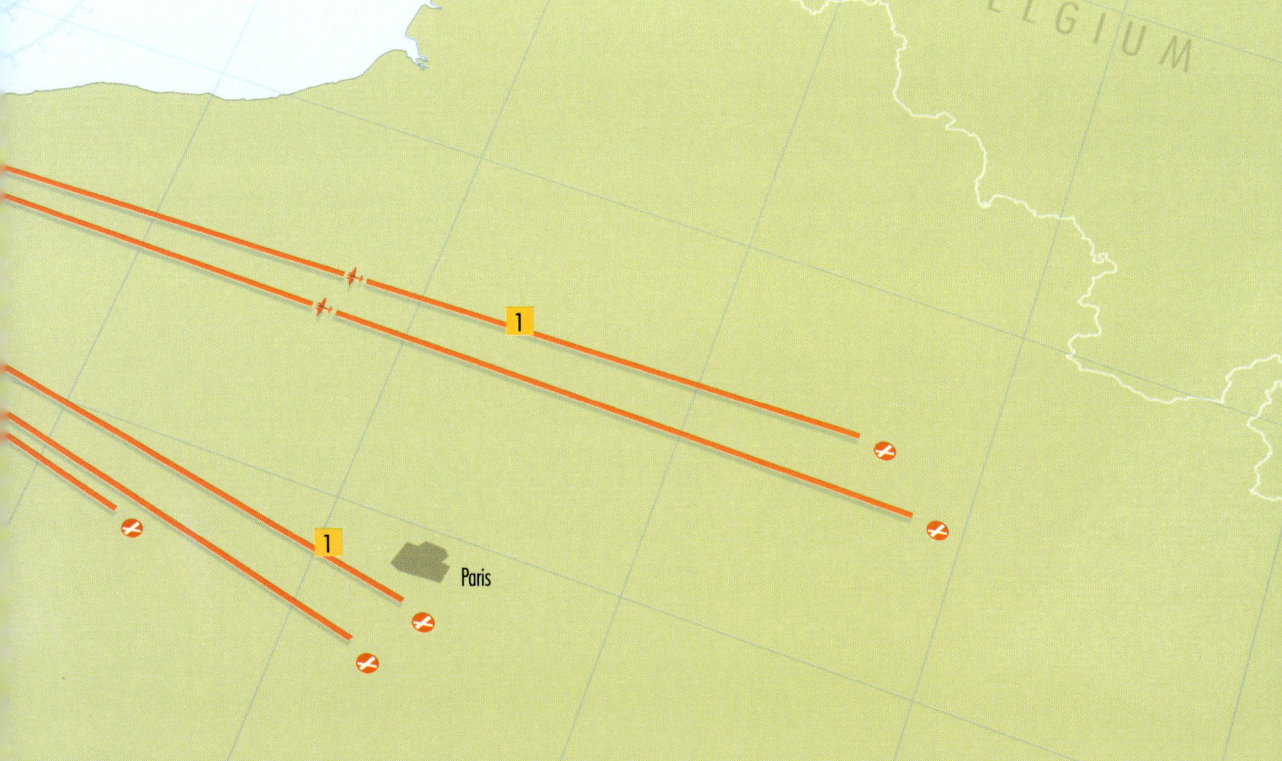

Desperation – April 1944

Apart from a Fernnachtjagd mission by II./KG 51 in the early hours of 31 March 1944, very little took place until the nights of 11 and 12 April 1944, when further intruder missions were carried out by II./KG 51 in addition to Störangriff against London by I./SKG 10 on the same night, as well as another Störangriff by I./SKG 10 on the night of 13 April 1944. Curiously, on the night of 6 April 1944, an unknown number of Ju 88As from Einsatzstaffel Verbandsführerschule/KG 101 operated over south-west England – precise targets were not recorded but one Ju 88 flown by Fw Johannes Günsch failed to return (no obvious British claims) while a second flown by Fw August Spoo was shot down by German Flak and crashed at St Saviour on Jersey.

The first major attack of the month did not come until the night of 18 April 1944 and again the target was London. Of considerable concern to the Luftwaffe was a much-reduced force, estimated by the British as being 58, crossing the coast, of which 53 made it to London, scattering their bombs over the capital with no clear target. Considering the number of aircraft attacking, losses were unusually high, and of those killed, a number were notable by their experience.

RAF nightfighters claimed nine aircraft destroyed, two probably destroyed and one damaged. Losses were 12 over England and another five either crashing on take-off or their return. Forty-one aircrew would lose their lives and 15 were captured. Those notable casualties were Hptm Helmut Eichbaum, Staffelkapitän of 4./KG 2 (his time in command lasted just a week), and Deutsches Kreuz in Gold holders Oblt Alfred Hein of 5./KG 2 and Oblt Richard Pahl, Staffelkapitän of 1./KG 51. Eichbaum had been flying operationally from September 1939 with 6./KG 3. Hein was a veteran of the Legion Condor and his Do 17 of 5./KG 2 was reported as being damaged in combat on 8 September 1940, and his Do 217 was reported damaged in combat on 18 November 1941 and 4 March 1942. By the time of his death, he had flown over 290 operational flights, and it was anticipated he would be awarded the Ritterkreuz. Pahl had flown operationally over the Soviet Union from May 1941 and received the Deutsches Kreuz in Gold in December 1943; he would be promoted to Hauptmann after his death – his Me 410 was shot down by Wg Cdr Ed Crew of 96 Sqn and crashed into a cemetery in Brighton. Eight crews from Einsatzstaffel Verbandsführerschule/KG 101 were reported attached to I./KG 54 for the attack this night, a probable sign of how short of aircraft and crews the Luftwaffe was becoming.

Oblt Alfred Hein's (5./KG 2, far left) luck would finally run out on the night of 18 April 1944, when his Ju 188 was shot down by Wg Cdr Charles Miller of 85 Sqn and crashed near Ivychurch in Kent. Hein had flown with the Legion Condor, after which he flew with 5./KG 2. His Do 17 was damaged by Flak on 8 September 1940, and then on 18 November 1941, his Do 217 crash-landed with engine trouble. On 4 March 1942, his Do 217 was damaged by Flak. In each case he was unwounded or uninjured. He would be awarded the Ehrenpokal and Deutsches Kreuz in Gold. His body lies today in Folkestone New Cemetery. (Author's collection)

The tail of Oblt Richard Pahl's Me 410A-1 of 1./KG 51 at St Nicholas Church, Brighton after having been shot down by Wg Cdr Ed Crew of 96 Sqn, 19 April 1944. Pahl was a highly experienced bomber pilot who had flown nearly all of his flights on the Eastern Front. (Andy Saunders)

The remainder of April 1944 was yet again an anti-climax as well as a continuation of needless Luftwaffe casualties. The night of 19 April saw 15 Me 410s of I./KG 51 carrying out a Störangriff against London, with one from 1./KG 51 being shot down by Flt Lt Clive Brooks of 456 Sqn near Horsham. The following night, around 60 aircraft headed for Hull failed to land a single bomb on the city but lost six aircraft during that attack, five returning damaged or being attacked by intruders. Again, one more experienced pilot was lost. Hptm Herbert Dostlebe, Staffelkapitän of 2./KG 100, had first started flying operationally with Fw

The 'Exbury Junkers', 0745hrs, Tuesday 18 April 1944

It was normal during *Steinbock* for German bombers to move to various bases away from their main operating base in preparation for attacks the same night. This is what is believed to have happened in the early hours of 18 April 1944, but with deadly consequences for a German crew.

Ju 188E-1 pathfinder of 2./KG 66 flown by Uffz Johann Czipin was apparently relocating from its base at Montdidier – there was no attack the previous night and the attack that night would be London, so where it was going cannot be said with any certainty, but it was believed to be Soesterberg in Holland. As a result, in addition to a crew of five, it was also carrying two groundcrew. However, instead of heading east towards Holland, at 0745hrs it was reported at 4,000ft off the Isle of Wight headed west.

Attracted by gunfire aimed at a twin-engined aircraft, four Typhoons of 266 Sqn based at RAF Tangmere near Chichester, led by Flt Lt Arthur Sanders and which were returning from an exercise, went to investigate. Sanders wrote of what happened next: 'I turned inside it to investigate it and confirmed it was a Ju 188. I experienced slight return fire from the e/a. Closing in, I opened fire at about 200yds with slight deflection from port side and saw strikes on cockpit and the port wing root followed by flames and smoke from this area. As I flew over e/a, I noticed pieces falling from it and next saw it burned on the ground with a large column of smoke rising from it.'

The kill was shared with Sanders' No. 2 Flt Sgt Don Dodd, and the German bomber crashed in flames at a shallow angle at Exbury House near Beaulieu in Hampshire, killing all on board. The 266 Sqn Operations Record book noted: 'On investigating the crash, it was found the aircraft carried a crew of seven and must have been lost in bad weather. Flt Lt Sanders and Flt Sgt Dodd thus destroyed the first Hun on English soil for 266.'

The Air Intelligence report further tried to explain what had happened: 'It was deemed remarkable that a crew of seven was carried. It is probable that the aircraft was flying a reciprocal course as two crew were groundcrew and therefore the machine was hopelessly lost due to thick ground mist.'

Rumours have abounded since the war that the crew were deserting but it now seems it was simply a compass error compounded by poor weather conditions that contributed to this aircraft and its crew's demise.

200s of 3./KG 40 on 16 March 1941. He was awarded the Ehrenpokal in April 1941 and on 20 April 1944, his He 177 was shot down into the North Sea by Fg Off John Corre of 264 Sqn. Fifteen Me 410s from II./KG 51 carried out intruder missions targeting airfields at Seething, Horsham St Faith and Lakenheath that night without noticeable success. However, the evening of 22 April 1944 would see a number of spectacular successes for II./KG 51, but they did again come at a cost.

Fourteen Me 410s of II./KG 51 presumably led by Ritterkreuz holder Hptm Dietrich Puttfarken, Staffelkapitän of 5./KG 51, carried out an intruder mission stated as being against the airfield at Rackham in Norfolk. That evening, American bombers were returning from an attack on Hamm and as the B-24 Liberators of the 2nd Bomb Division, located at the rear of the bomber stream, approached the Norfolk coast, the German intruders pounced. Between 2204 and 2246hrs, the intruders claimed 12 of what they thought were Halifaxes. Successful pilots with confirmed claims were Lt Wolfgang Wenning Stab II./KG 51, Hptm Werner Duero 4./KG 51, Lt Uwe Laas 5./KG 51, Fw Johann Trenke 6./KG 51 (three), Uffz Eberhard Baier 6./KG 51 (three) and Wenning's Bordfunker Fw Gustav Delp 6./KG 51. The 389th Bomb Group (BG) lost one B-24, the 448th BG lost four, the 453rd BG and 458th BG one each and the 467th BG two; a number of bombers were also badly damaged in their haste to land. Of the successful aircrew, Wenning, Duero, Laas and Delp would all be killed in 1944, while Trenke would be awarded the Deutsches Kreuz in Gold and Ritterkreuz later in the year, and survived the war only to be killed in a flying accident in 1957.

Despite these successes, the German fighters did not get off without loss – the Me 410 flown by Oblt Klaus Krüger of 6./KG 51 was mortally damaged by return fire from a B-24 from either the 389th or 467th BG and crashed at Ashby St Mary, his plane exploding and killing him and his Bordfunker, while the Me 410 flown by Puttfarken simply disappeared. The losses of both crews would have had a serious detrimental effect on the operational efficiency of II./KG 51 – all four aircrew killed this night had been awarded the Deutsches Kreuz in Gold and Ehrenpokal for previous service with KG 51 on the Eastern Front. The intruders would return again after midnight that night and Uffz Walter Brügel of 4./KG 51 shot down an Albermarle of 42 Operational Training Unit (OTU) on a night navigation exercise.

The following night, another attack on Bristol took place, the British reporting, tongue in cheek:

The Do 217K-2 and K-3 flown by III./KG 100 had enlarged wings so they could carry Fritz X guided bombs. This type of bomb was only used against mainland Britain once when the aim was to hit warships at Plymouth on 30 April 1944. (Author's collection)

On the night of 23/24 April a bombing attack developed on the Poole–Bournemouth area and on the following day the German radio broadcast a claim that a concentrated attack had been made on Bristol. No bombs whatever fell in the Bristol area on this night and it at first seemed possible that the Luftwaffe had switched its target at the last moment but had forgotten to inform its propaganda department which consequently applied its usual grandiose claim to the wrong objective. From interrogation of the three survivors from 4D+FM it is apparently that the target for II and III./KG 30 at least was certainly Bristol and the fact that no bombs fell on that city must once more be attributed to the incompetence of the bomber or pathfinder arm of the Luftwaffe.

Incompetent or not, ten bombers failed to return and another three crashed on their return. One lost was from the inexperienced Einsatzstaffel Verbandsführerschule/KG 101.

The next attack was against a new target, namely Portsmouth in Hampshire on the night of 25 April 1944, and again it was ineffectual with a mixed bag of casualties – an Fw 190G-3, a Ju 188, a Do 217M-1, a Ju 88S-1, an He 177A-3 and two Me 410s. The Me 410s were from 1.(F)/121 carrying out photoreconnaissance and were shot down by 85 Sqn, Flt Lt Branse Burbidge being responsible for the demise of the aircraft flown by Oblt Hermann Kroll, an experienced reconnaissance pilot who had been awarded the Ritterkreuz for his efforts over the Soviet Union.

The Luftwaffe visited Portsmouth once more on the night of 26 April, causing little if no damage to the city but again losing four bombers during the mission, with two crashing on the return, one being flown by Hptm Gustav Heckewerth, the new Staffelkapitän of just

Loss of Do 217 K-3, 6N+IT, Plymouth raid, 30 April 1944

In darkness on the morning of 29 April 1944, 15 Do 217s of III./KG 100, each carrying a single Fritz X, took off from Toulouse-Francazal in south-west France for Orleans, where they met up with their Kommandeur Hptm Herbert Pfeffer. That afternoon, the crews were briefed as to their target and tactics, but the problem would be that the crews were not used to dropping Fritz X at night let alone on a combat mission, and for many crews, including Hptm Pfeffer, this would be their first operational mission with the bomb. Recent reconnaissance photographs had shown a King George V-class battleship (HMS *Howe*) lying north to south in a basin to the east side of the Hamoaze, the estuary that flows past Devonport Naval Dockyard, as well as another battleship and a cruiser nearby.

No more than 12 aircraft then took off from Orleans that night and headed to Morlaix in Brittany, where they would pick up the Knickebein blind bombing beam and head for Plymouth. They would then use the same beam to head back for Toulouse after the attack. The target was meant to be illuminated by I./KG 66 however, it would appear they were late or the Do 217s early, as when the first aircraft arrived over Plymouth at 0330hrs, no flares were seen. Furthermore, a mist and a smoke screen further obscured Plymouth. Minimal damage was inflicted on Plymouth let alone the warships. A Ju 88 from 5./KG 6, another from 9./KG 54 and an Fw 190 from 3./SKG 10, were lost over the Channel while a second Fw 190 from 3./SKG 10 crashed near St-Brieuc in Brittany. Two claims were submitted for Ju 88s by 68 Sqn for one probably destroyed off Morlaix and 406 Sqn for another destroyed south of Start Point.

In addition, two Do 217s were also lost – the Do 217K-3 flown by Lt Herbert Palme of 9./KG 100 was the fourth aircraft to take off from Orleans, but as he approached Plymouth, his ailerons apparently jammed. He then made a guess at where his target was and the bomb dropped, but shortly after, his plane was illuminated by searchlights and blinded and Palme lost control, the aircraft went into a spin and he crashed near Totnes in Devon. The second was a Do 217K-2 which was flown by the Kommandeur. On reaching the target area the crew could see nothing, so orbited four times, during which the bomber was illuminated by searchlights, the pilot blinded and the starboard engine set on fire. The bomb was jettisoned, and the crew attempted to bale out, but Pfeffer and his observer were killed when the bomber crashed south of Plymouth, two of the crew surviving – one being captured by American soldiers south of St Germans in Cornwall, the other being rescued from the sea at 0645hrs at Portwrinkle also in Cornwall. Although the German survivors thought they had been shot down by Flak or had lost control, Sqn Ldr David Williams of 406 Sqn was credited with two Do 217s.

The Luftwaffe had boasted that 400 aircraft took part in this attack but, in reality, it was more like 30–35 aircraft according to the British. The alert had sounded at 0315hrs and lasted 70 minutes. No ships were sunk but it appears that one Fritz X 'fell right in the centre of the [Plymouth] Gas Company's recreation ground, it simply left a huge crater without causing any damage to the tremendous collection of vehicles and other war materials assembled around the fringe of the ground'.

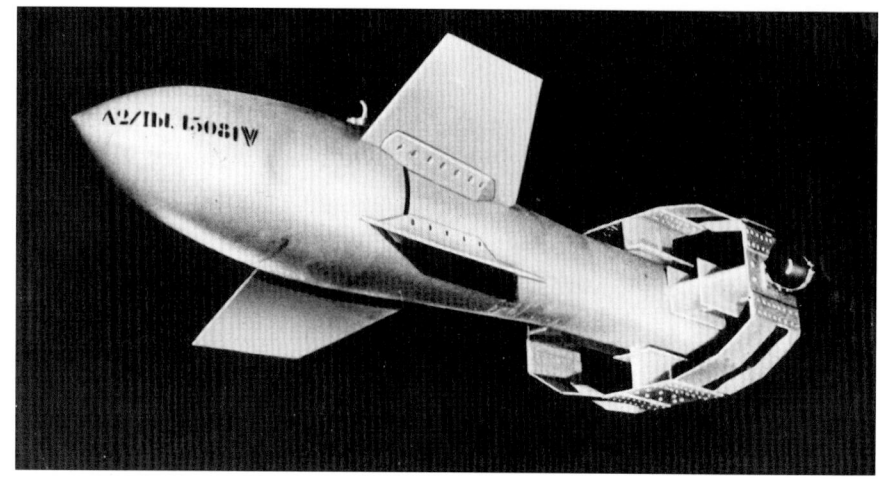

What III./KG 100 dropped on Plymouth in the early hours of 30 April 1944 – the PC1400 Fritz X. Apart from some large craters, the attack was a failure and resulted in a number of losses. (Author's collection)

a week of 2./KG 100, who with three of his crew was killed. This appears to be the end of I./KG 100 operations, as a few days later, its He 177s moved to Fassberg, where it was redesignated III./KG 1; it would then be disbanded in August 1944. The He 177s of I and II./KG 40 still would not be seen on operations until 7 June 1944, following the Allied invasion of Normandy.

This night saw another intruder victory and loss when Lt Wolfgang Wenning of Stab II./KG 51 collided with an Oxford of 18 (Pilots) Advanced Flying Unit flown by Plt Off Gregor Moore; both aircraft crashed at Frankton near Rugby, killing the three aircrew.

The remainder of April 1944 saw a single Ju 88A of 4./KG 6 being lost minelaying in the early hours of 29 April 1944, when pilot error saw the bomber hit the sea and sink, taking three of the four crew with it, the Bordfunker surviving.

The last attack of the month came on the night of 29 April and was different to *Steinbock* attacks before and after, as it saw Do 217s of III./KG 100 launching Fritz X guided bombs against warships in Plymouth. The target was meant to be illuminated by I./KG 66, but it would appear they were late or the Do 217s of III./KG 100 early, as when the first aircraft arrived over Plymouth at 0330hrs, no flares were seen. Furthermore, a mist and a smoke screen further obscured Plymouth. What happened afterwards is that minimal damage was inflicted on Plymouth let alone the warships. A Ju 88 from 5./KG 6 (flown by Uffz Eberhard Bernsdorf) and another from 9./KG 54 (flown by Uffz Hubert Bach) and an Fw 190 from 3./SKG 10 (flown by Lt Herbert Möller) were lost over the Channel, while a second Fw 190 flown by Ofw Hans Lüders of 3./SKG 10 crashed near St-Brieuc in Brittany. Two claims were submitted for Ju 88s by Flt Lt Josef Kapka of 68 Sqn for one probably destroyed off Morlaix, and 1st/Lt Stanley Kvam of 406 Sqn for another destroyed south of Start Point. However, there were another two significant losses that night. The Do 217K-3 flown by Lt Herbert Palme of 9./KG 100 and the Do 217K-2 flown by the Kommandeur Hptm Herbert Pfeffer were shot down by Sqn Ldr David 'Blackie' Williams and his Nav/Rad Fg Off Clarence 'Kirk' Kirkpatrick of 406 Sqn, the former bomber crashing on land, the latter crashing in the sea.

Lt Herbert Möller of 3./SKG 10, who failed to return from the attack on Plymouth on the night of 29–30 April 1944. The reason for his loss is not known, as no Fw 190s were claimed by AA or fighters that night. (Author's collection)

The German propaganda had boasted that 400 aircraft took part in the Plymouth attack but in reality, it was more like 30–35 aircraft according to the British, while surviving German records state it was more like 101 aircraft from IX Fliegerkorps.

Futile final month – May 1944

The first two weeks of May 1944 were unusually quiet, with no operational losses over Britain. Even the intruders were quiet – Fw Hermann Bolten of 4./KG 51 recorded just the one Fernnachtjagd mission on the night of 8 May 1944, while Einsatzstaffel Verbandsführerschule/KG 101 would lose its final Ju 88 on an unspecified mission on 7 May 1944.

The first major attack of the month was against Bristol on the night of 14 May 1944 by all available crews from KG 2, I./KG 6, II./KG 30, I./KG 51, I./KG 54; pathfinding was performed by five Me 410s from II./KG 51 and seven Ju 88S/Ju 188s from I./KG 66. As with the previous two attacks on Bristol, this again was another futile effort by the Luftwaffe, not helped by the pathfinders being late and not marking the target correctly. Luftflotte 3 stated that 91 aircraft participated (while German propaganda said 150!); British assessments were that around 80 crossed the coast, penetrated parts of southern and south-west England and that the attack was 'scattered and ragged'. The attack on Bristol was preceded by Störangriff attacks by I./SKG 10 against coastal towns between Portland and Bournemouth. The Luftwaffe for the first time tried to use Kettenhund jammers against British radar, 44 aircraft from KG 2 having already been fitted with this equipment, and 13 of these aircraft were used this night. Kettenhund was to be switched on 80km before reaching the coast and switched off 80km after crossing the coast, but the effect of jamming from a German point of view, seemed 'not to have been satisfactory'. The RAF noted that there was jamming from both the German air and ground stations at Boulogne and Cap Gris-Nez, but there was never a total block of ground radar, while there was no noted effect against gun-laying radar and AI sets.

One pilot taking part was Oblt Karl von Manowarda, Staffelkapitän of 1./KG 6, another highly experienced bomber pilot the Luftwaffe could ill afford to lose. His operational career started on 15 October 1940 flying Do 17s with 5./KG 2. He then flew in Russia, became an instructor with 11./KG 2 (during which time he flew during the Baedeker Blitz), then flew Do 217s with Stab I./KG 2 (where on 24 June 1942, he had his first encounter with an RAF nightfighter when his Bordmechaniker was killed) then 3./KG 2 (where he had his second encounter with an RAF nightfighter on 4 January 1943, when his Bordfunker was wounded). In May 1943, he was posted to command 1./KG 6, converting from the Ju 88A-14 to the Ju 188E-1 by October 1943. His third encounter with a nightfighter in the early hours of 15 May 1944 was not so lucky:

> Hampshire-there I had my first parachute jump. Shot down in flames at 6300m height by a Mosquito. I had been flying with [anti-collision] lights on which my Beobachter had switched on in error. Searchlights had passed us on and on. The nightfighter's first burst hit home. Port engine burnt at once.
>
> I landed softly in a freshly ploughed field, wearing only socks as my flying boots had flown off. It was hard getting rid of my parachute as I had burns to my hands and face and I had a broken arm. Walking along a street [at Selbourne] I came to a small house and cried "Hello!" A man with a lamp spoke to me from the inside and asked me to go to the back of the house. He then left the house using the front door and ran into the village. Two Home Guardsmen then disarmed me and took me to the mayor. There I was shocked by my wounds and very politely I was directed to lie down on a divan. At once a young housewife, kneeling in front of me, began bandaging my burnt hands most gently …

Oblt Karl Von Manowarda, who commanded 1./KG 6 and was shot down by Flt Lt Charles Ramsey of 264 Sqn, 15 May 1944. This pilot had begun his operational career in October 1940; his Do 217 had been badly damaged by RAF nightfighters twice before and his violent manoeuvres trying to get away from the 264 Sqn Mosquito resulted in the loss of the Mosquito. (Author's collection)

The then 12-year-old Phil Barber remembers the night clearly:

> When the German airman baled out, he landed in a field between the villages of Newton Valence and Selbourne. He then managed to reach the two cottages on the outskirts of Selbourne where he awoke Bill Cummings, a local cowman. Bill then went next door to arouse his neighbour, Eric Woolhead, a Sgt in the Home Guard who came around in uniform also with his rifle which caused quite a laugh with the villagers for quite a while as the poor fellow was in no state to put up a fight …

Von Manowarda and his Bordfunker were the only two survivors, the aircraft disintegrating over West Worldham in Hampshire, one of its two 1,000kg bombs landing alongside the village church but not exploding (a memorial to this can still be seen in the church). The Ju 188 was shot down by a Mosquito of 264 Sqn flown by Flt Lt Charles Ramsey DFC with Fg Off Johnnie Edgar DFC his Nav/Rad. The combat was not as straightforward as it might have seemed:

> … I could see a large intersection of beams and gauntleted in dive towards the intersection and when two miles away saw e/a taking violent evasive action in searchlight beam coming towards me on north-easterly course. I turned to starboard and then turning to port closed in behind and at one mile range obtained contact. E/a commenced steep diving weave; as I closed in behind I identified e/a as a Ju 88 or 188 by general appearance.
>
> At 300yds range and at 14,000ft height, I opened fire with 10–15 degrees angle off, half ring deflection but no strikes seen. E/a then jettisoned incendiaries. Second burst given with 2–3 rings deflection, angle off at 150yds range on target still doing diving turns. E/a immediately caught fire in cockpit, wing roots and starboard engine. I tried to drop back without success and I saw starboard wing of e/a break off at engine just before I passed over him at approximately 12,000ft. No return fire was seen …

Mosquito NF XIII of 264 Sqn seen at RAF Hartford Bridge, May 1944. Originally a Boulton Paul Defiant squadron at the start of the war, it was the first squadron to convert to the Mosquito and ended the war flying from Rheine in Germany. (Author's collection)

However, for the two RAF crew, this flight was about to end dramatically and for one of them, tragically:

> … I was now in a very steep dive. Gyros had toppled and the searchlights doused so I tried to recover on the remaining instruments by easing the stick back. The altimeter continued to show a very rapid loss of height. I then saw the ground by the lights of the burning e/a and I was diving vertically down. I gave the order to bale out. I increased the backward pressure on the control column when about halfway out of the dive, something broke. The "G" stopped, the controls became slack and the radio dead, the speed dropped off and the aircraft went into a spin. The observer jettisoned the door and appeared to be getting out. For some time he was crouching near the door and I thought he may have been having difficulty in getting his parachute on. As I was very near to the ground and there was nothing I could do, I decided to try and get out of the top hatch which I accomplished successfully after a short struggle. As I left the aircraft, I hit the tail. On pulling the rip cord, the parachute opened immediately and at the same time I saw the aircraft hit the ground and burst into flames. I landed at the edge of a ploughed field and ran to the crash which was 400yds away but I could not see any sign of the observer.

Sadly, Johnny Edgar failed to get out and was killed.

It was another dreadful night of losses for the Germans – 11 aircraft failed to return with another two crashing in France; 42 men were killed and nine captured for no tactical, strategic or even revenge benefit. Furthermore, an attack the following night by a similar number of aircraft against Portsmouth again saw 'no appreciable harm' done but saw four aircraft failing to return, with all 17 crew killed; *Steinbock* was on the verge of fizzling out. In respect of this Bristol attack, Luftflotte 3 wrote afterwards:

> Attacks on dark nights can only be carried out successfully if the faultless operation of the pathfinders is guaranteed. The present procedure employed can no longer be used with assurance because of extensive and effective enemy jamming. Further attacks on the targets in the Bristol Channel, which are difficult from the weather point of view, therefore only give promise of success, till enemy jamming is overcome, in adequate light conditions, i.e. moonlight, in which case still higher losses must be put up with.

Pilots from I./SKG 10. Few would survive the war, including Fw Otto Heinrich, 2nd from left. He would be reported missing attacking Portsmouth on the night of 22 May 1944, his body later being washed ashore in France. He would be awarded the Ritterkreuz posthumously. (Author's collection)

OPPOSITE MAP OF *STEINBOCK* BOMBING RESULTS

It would now prove to be a disappointing end for *Steinbock*. An attack against Portsmouth on 22 May 1944 by about 75 aircraft again accomplished nothing apart from more German bloodletting, with 125 and 456 Sqn each claiming four aircraft destroyed off the coast. Seven aircraft were lost including two of note. One was Fw 190G-3 of 3./SKG 10 flown by Fw Otto Heinrich. Heinrich had been awarded the Deutsches Kreuz in Gold with 8./St.G 77 in October 1942. His body would later be washed ashore in France, and he would be awarded the Ritterkreuz posthumously. The second lost was another Deutsches Kreuz in Gold winner, the Geschwader Kommodore of KG 2 Maj Wilhelm Rath. Twenty-nine-year-old Rath was a pre-war bomber pilot who had then flown with KG 51 almost without a break before being appointed Kommodore of KG 2 in April 1944. It was a curious twist of fate that, as a member of Stab III./KG 51, on 12 August 1940, he together with Oblt Grassmann, Uffz Kurt Böttcher and Gefr Michael Gallermann, had taken part in the first major daylight attack on Portsmouth in the Battle of Britain.

There would be three more *Steinbock* attacks of the campaign, all against coastal targets in the west of England, all of which were connected with the build-up of forces for the invasion of Normandy. The first was against Weymouth on the night of 27 May 1944 by 20 aircraft, while another 40 would drop mines between Weymouth and Portland at the same time; four civilians were killed in Weymouth. Then it was Torquay's turn on the night of 28 May, when 65 aircraft from KG 2 and KG 6 bombed the town and mined Torbay. Hptm Erwin Lissat of 2./KG 6 was the only German loss; the reason for his demise is not certain, as the only nightfighter claim that night, by 68 Sqn, was later believed to have resulted in the shooting down of a Mosquito of 604 Sqn flown by Flt Lt Cliff Harris just north of Start Point. Thirty-one-year-old Lissat was a pre-war Stuka pilot who, after being captured in the Poland Campaign, had spent much of the war instructing on He 111s with KG 27. Bombs were recorded landing on Park Crescent, The Bay Court Hotel, Park Place, Victoria Park Road and Bronshill Road; 20 civilians were recorded as losing their lives with another 33 injured.

The final attack of *Steinbock* was by 50 aircraft from KG 2 and KG 6 bombing and mining Falmouth Harbour on the night of 29 May 1944. The lead aircraft dropped red and green flares to mark the target as well as Düppel, and the bombers then came across the Carrick Roads, the Docks and the Castle Promontory, along the seafront to Swanpool and across the

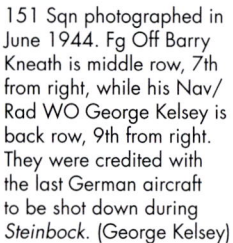

151 Sqn photographed in June 1944. Fg Off Barry Kneath is middle row, 7th from right, while his Nav/Rad WO George Kelsey is back row, 9th from right. They were credited with the last German aircraft to be shot down during *Steinbock*. (George Kelsey)

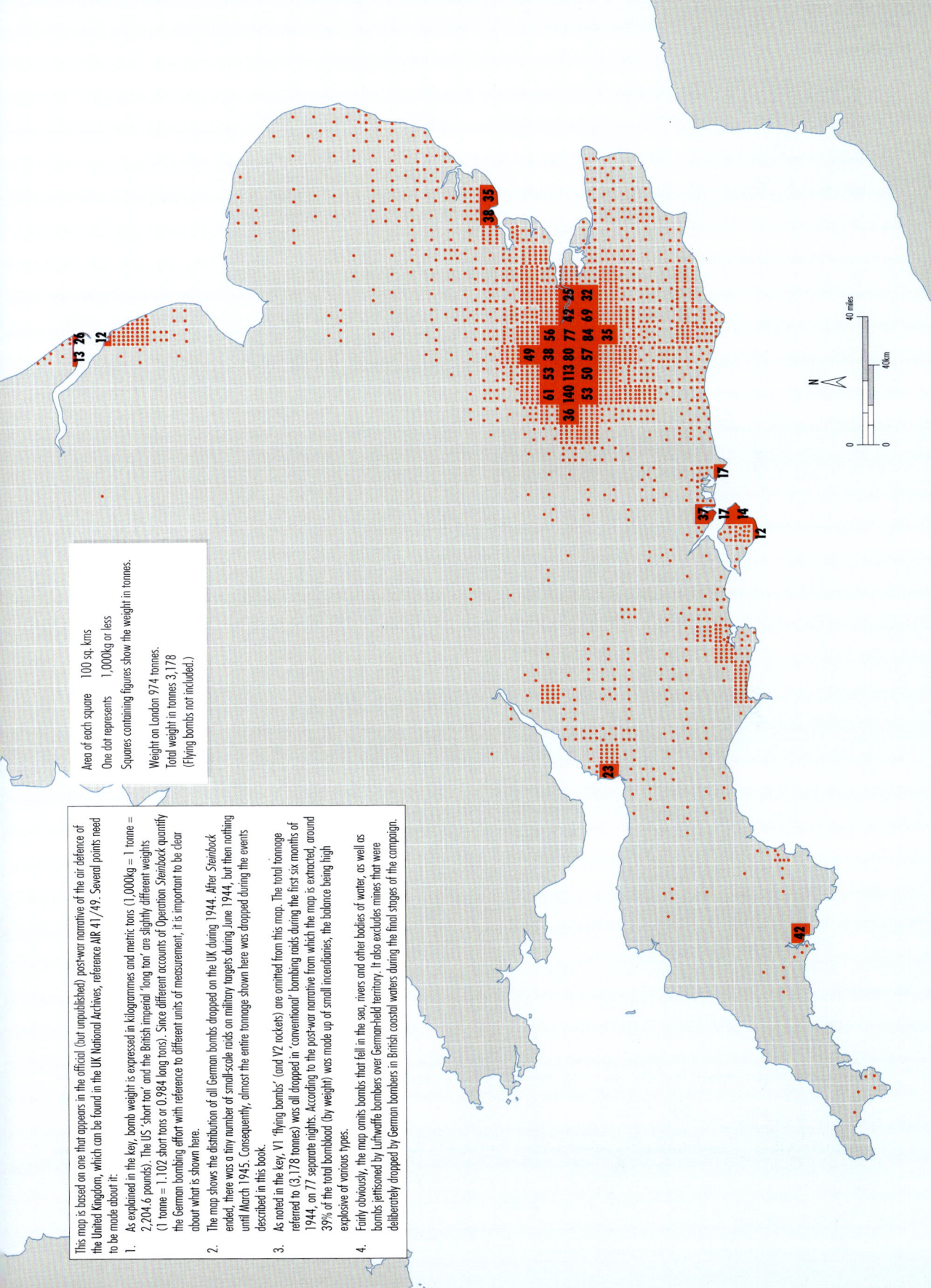

Major Wilhelm Rath, Kommodore of KG 2, who was lost attacking Portsmouth on 22 May 1944. A highly experienced pilot who had been awarded the Ehrenpokal and Deutsches Kreuz in Gold, receiving the latter for 216 operational flights. He had only been in command of KG 2 since 12 April 1944. (Author's collection)

River Helford. One of the huge storage tanks at the Swanvale Oil Installation, carefully camouflaged in the hillside above Swanpool and containing 1,250,000 gallons of fuel, received a direct hit. Two tanks were set on fire and the side of Tank 3 was blown out, and escaping fuel flowed down towards the village of Swanpool, where residents had to be evacuated while American servicemen cut channels with a bulldozer and successfully built dams to retain fuel for which two Americans, one of them Bosun's Mate Philip Bishop, were awarded the British Empire Medal. Several hotels on the seafront were hit and three civilians lost their lives – Charles Etches (71), Violet Fox (63) and Louise Harland (82) were all killed at the Pentargan Hotel, Cliff Road. Fg Off Barry Kneath of 151 Sqn claimed to have shot down an He 111 ten miles south of Falmouth but the only loss was Lt Kurt Nieymayer and his crew from 5./KG 6. Barry Kneath's claim, together with his Nav/Rad Flt Sgt George Kelsey, would be the last nightfighter victories of *Steinbock*; George Kelsey wrote what happened:

A few days before D-Day there was an attack on Falmouth, I think as part of investigative bombing raids on the south coast. On 29 May 1944 I was re-crewed with Fg Off Kneath (my usual pilot Flt Sgt Jack Playford was on rest) and our first night patrol at 2359hrs led us to the interception of a He 111 [sic] approaching Falmouth (20 miles away) where oil tanks were burning. He was shot down, our aircraft having wheels and flaps down to prevent stalling at the time of shooting.

The combat report for the last air combat of *Steinbock* was very short and to the point:

Was ordered to investigate bogeys five miles south-east. Immediately amended to hostile at 2,000ft travelling north. After a few more vectors contact was obtained three miles head-on. Turned under target onto target's course. Closed in rapidly through Window and overshot. Carried out overshoot procedure and regained contact at 1½ miles. Bandit was climbing taking mild evasive action and dropping Window. Visual obtained at 2,000ft. Height 4,000ft. Closed to 200ft directly below and identified a He 111 [sic]. Throttled back to dead astern and opened fire with a short burst from 300ft. Port engine of He 111 blew up and aircraft dived steeply, emitting flames and debris, hitting the sea in a large explosion.

On 14 July 1944, the remains of what was identified as Uffz Erich Schwartz, the gunner, were found in the sea south of the Isle of Wight. The last victor of *Steinbock*, Barry Kneath, would lose his life on 11 December 1952 flying with 616 Sqn when his Meteor collided with another flown by Flt Lt John Harland 23 miles north-east of Whitby, while George Kelsey passed away peacefully in 2013.

The three civilians and four German aircrew would therefore be the last casualties of Operation *Steinbock* as seven days later, the Allies landed in Normandy and German attentions turned to France.

Postscript

If the bombers were having little success, a small number of intruders from II./KG 51 had been active on the nights of 21, 22, 24, 28 and 31 May and 1 and 5 June 1944, and achieved some successes, I./KG 51 by now having been withdrawn from the front line in preparation

Crews from KG 2 preparing for an attack on London during *Steinbock*; few would survive *Steinbock* let alone the war. (Split)

for conversion to the Me 262. On the plus side, on 22 May 1944, Uffz Ebehard Baier of 6./KG 51 shot down the Lancaster of 619 Sqn flown by Fg Off Bob Redshaw at East Wretham. Baier would be credited with one more while Fw Johann Trenke of 6./KG 51 was credited with another three. The following night, a Lancaster of 582 Sqn flown by Sqn Ldr Harold Heney reported being attacked by an intruder near Little Staughton, while an Anson of 13 OTU flown by Fg Off Paul Davidson was attacked by an intruder at around the same time and location, Davidson being mortally wounded by a 20mm round. Two 105 Sqn Mosquitoes were also damaged on the ground at RAF Bourn. The final claim for the month was again by Baier, who on 29 May 1944 shot down a Stirling of 1657 Conversion Unit flown by Fg Off Bill Yates, which then crashed onto another two Stirlings at RAF Stradishall. On the minus side, two Me 410s from 5./KG 51 collided on take-off from Gilze-Rijen on 29 May 1944, killing two and injuring two, while Wg Cdr Mike Wight-Boycott of 25 Sqn shot down the Me 410 flown by Fw Ernst Dietrich of 6./KG 51 off Cromer at 0336hrs on the same day. It is of note that the first German casualty of D-Day was an Me 410A-1/U2 of 4./KG 51 shot down by Fg Off Roy Lelong of 605 Sqn at 0148hrs on 6 June 1944, landing at St André and which crashed at Marcilly-la-Campagne, killing Bordfunker Fw Wilhelm Lohf and wounding the highly experienced Me 210/410 pilot Ofw Hermann Bolten, who never again flew operationally. II./KG 51 would itself be withdrawn from operations in August 1944 and the following month would also start converting to the Me 262.

The Fw 190s of I./SKG 10 were also stated as attacking Portsmouth on the night of 29 May, Bournemouth on 1 June, London on 3 June and Portsmouth on 5 June. However, if they did, they had little or no effect, as on the morning of 6 June 1944, *Steinbock* was well and truly over. Again of note, the first German claims for Allied aircraft shot down on 6 June 1944 were from I./SKG 10, when Oblt Helmut Eberspächer and Fw Kurt Eisele of 3./SKG 120 claimed three Lancasters in the Isigny/Lessay/Carentan area of which three, two from 97 Sqn and one from 50 Sqn, can be matched with their claims.

Mosquito NF XIII of 96 Sqn showing its distinctive Thimble nose for the Airborne Interception (AI) Mk. VIII. 96 Sqn was based at RAF West Malling near Maidstone in Kent. (Author's collection)

ANALYSIS AND CONCLUSION

Overview

At 0415hrs on 13 June 1944, exactly seven days after the Allies landed in Normandy, ten V1 'pilotless aircraft' were reported headed towards London. Two reached London, destroying the railway bridge at Grove Road, Bethnal Green and killing six civilians and injuring another nine seriously; a further 13 appeared over Folkestone 45 minutes later. The new phase of the attack against mainland Britain had begun. However, if the Luftwaffe bomber force was expecting things to be better over the Normandy beaches, they were gravely mistaken. With Allied day and night air superiority, it soon became a slaughter. By means of example, KG 6 lost three Gruppen Kommandeur and Ritterkreuzträger in quick succession – Hptm Johann Thurner, Kommandeur of I./KG 6, was killed in action on 11 June 1944, Maj Rudolf Puchinger, Kommandeur of III./KG 6, was killed in action on 13 June 1944, and Maj Johann Mader Kommandeur of II./KG 6 was killed in combat on 3 July 1944. Even the Geschwader Kommodore of KG 6, Oberst Hermann Hogeback, was shot down on 4 August 1944, but he and his crew were uninjured and landed behind German lines.

As one German historian has stated, the Luftwaffe's performance in *Steinbock* could be regarded as pathetic. Planning a campaign at such short notice with the single target, at the start, of London was fraught with danger and difficulty, and when targets then moved to ports, their effectiveness with a depleted bomber force was negligible. That said, in the region of 1,569 civilians lost their lives during *Steinbock*, with another 2,916 seriously injured, over half of them occurring in London in February 1944. On 19 March 1944, Wg Cdr (later Sir) Eric Hodsoll, Inspector General of Civil Defence in the Ministry of Home Security, wrote:

> The population are more jittery than they were in the old days due probably to a lot of contributory factors such as belief that we had air superiority and therefore no more attacks to fear; war-weariness; lack of stamina and so on. There were no signs of any panic but the people seemed more helpless and more dependent on the Civil Defences services than they were in the old days …

A source of great irritation to the Luftwaffe – a searchlight in action. Once coned, German bombers like their Allied counterparts would be forced to fly erratically and violently to get out of the beam before AA could target them. (Author's collection, courtesy of the late K. Wakefield).

It is interesting to note that the British had also noted that blast damage from bombs dropped on London had increased considerably. This was because of the use of bombs containing Trialen, the so-called 'England Mix' of 70% TNT, 15% RDX and 15% aluminium powder. However, shortages of the aluminium powder soon restricted the blast effect of such bombs, little succour to those on which the bombs were being dropped, as the Borough of Islington noted:

> From a total of 12 bombs of various sizes that were dropped in the Borough, they have had to deal with 3,000 houses damaged or destroyed. This includes all houses which have had repairs done on them even if it was only glass. One incident involved a total of 500 houses damaged in varying degrees.

German inexperience?

Surprisingly, there was initially no shortage of trained aircrew, the Luftwaffe's aircrew training having ramped up considerably towards the end of 1943. However, there was a distinct mix of highly experienced aircrew, some of which had flown operationally throughout the war, and highly inexperienced aircrew. For example, Fw Günther Parge of 4./KG 6 flew his first Feindflug on the first night of *Steinbock*, taking part in the first wave between 1930 and 2345hrs and then the second wave between 0300 and 0625hrs – quite a baptism of fire. Parge's Gruppen Kommandeur was Hptm Johann Mader, who had joined the Luftwaffe in 1936, flying in the west with 4./KG 54 after which he flew on in the Battle of France, Battle of Britain, Blitz and then the Eastern Front, until returning to the west in July 1942, being awarded the Ritterkreuz in September 1942 after his 200th mission. He was then responsible for bringing into service the Ju 188 and assumed command of II./KG 6 in December 1943. He was only 28 at the time of *Steinbock*. However, pilots with the experience like Mader were rare and even then, their experience did not save them.

Furthermore, German morale might have been high at the start of *Steinbock*, but confidence soon began to flag, and British intelligence noted:

> Captured German airmen, to use their own words, "Haben die Schnauze voll" (have had a belly-full) and they are beginning to realise that their attacks, though larger and more sustained, are having no real effect on London.

Its crew being lost following being damaged by Flak over London, this Ju 88A-4 of 3./KG 54 landed at RAF Bradwell Bay in Essex at 0234hrs on 19 April 1944. Uffz Heinz Brandt and his crew had lost their bearings and when they landed at Bradwell Bay thought they were over the Continent. (Author's collection)

Navigation/Pathfinding

It had become clear that by 1943, the Germans had to develop a form of pathfinding to enable a more highly concentrated bombing pattern, something the Allies were already employing with great effect. Using navigational equipment and flares, and usually employing five aircraft to do all of this, invariably did not achieve the results they wanted (especially when the pathfinders were shot down) and on many occasions, targets were sporadically bombed or in the case of Bristol, not bombed at all despite German propaganda stating the contrary. For example, Luftflotte 3's analysis of this attack on 14–15 May 1944 had stated:

> Failure of the main operation is attributed to the unsuccessful pathfinder operation. Bombing was done by straight navigation because of the lack of illumination at the time of attack and the imprecise placing of flare bombs. It was appreciated that present procedure for attacks on dark nights could no longer be employed "with assurance", because of extensive and effective jamming.

Even the German use of jamming was ineffective – in addition to using Düppel, they also used Kettenhund jammers on the 14 May 1944 Bristol attack, reporting afterwards:

> With 13 Kettenhund aircraft operating, the total of losses (11) [from the whole force] is strikingly high. Orders were given to switch on the apparatus from 80km before to 80km after crossing the coast of the South of England. About the effect, nothing can be said.

To add to their woes, navigation, especially by inexperienced aircrew, was assessed as being poor. Despite having navigation equipment, it was turned off in case nightfighters detected the radar or was not trusted, with crew relying on Dead Reckoning. This relied on accurate weather forecasting and an ability to pick up beacons or see notable landmarks. Obviously, in poor weather conditions, this made the task of accurate navigation much harder. By means of example, the crew from 3./KG 54 who landed at RAF Bradwell Bay on 19 April 1944 had taken off from Wittmundhafen in northern Germany but, having then been damaged by Flak approaching London, the engine finally caught fire. In the confusion, the crew lost their bearings – instead of heading for a point to the east of Paris and then back to Wittmundhafen, they force-landed on an airfield in Essex, not on the Continent as they had thought.

Defences

The British and in particular the RAF had four years of honing its defences. The Mosquito was a superlative nightfighter, assisted by the latest AI and GCI radars. Anti-aircraft defences were now radar-assisted and located in such a way as to provide an effective ring of steel around major cities, especially London. Furthermore, RAF intruders were further limiting German bomber effectiveness. As an example, again, for the night of 14 May 1944, the Order of Battle was further reduced by 15 aircraft at the time of take-off on account of attacks on the bases of KG 2, KG 51 and KG 54.

Equipment

Most of the German aircraft used were suitable for the task. However, there were a number of weaknesses or shortfalls. First and foremost, despite the He 177 at last being ready for operations, only 1 and 2./KG 40 and 3./KG 100 were initially operational and even then, suffered heavily from losses both over England and back in France, accidents and unserviceability. Even though 1 and 2./KG 40 were withdrawn from *Steinbock* in early February 1944 and 2./KG 100 finally joined 3./KG 100, I./KG 100 was itself withdrawn from *Steinbock* at the end of April 1944. Second, the Fw 190 was superlative as a fighter or Jagdbomber, but being used at night put great pressures on the single pilot, and flying to London was described by some of them as like flying into hell. Furthermore, what could a single bomb add to the attack, and as the Kommandeur of I./SKG 10, Maj Kurt Dahlmann, wrote after the war, the efforts by his Gruppe 'were little more than a drop in the ocean'. Although there were the latest variants of Ju 88s, some units still flew the Ju 88A-4, which had first been seen over Britain in the summer of 1940. Finally, the Do 217 was becoming obsolete. It had almost single-handedly kept the offensive over Britain going from summer 1941 to autumn 1943 but was now being replaced by the Ju 188 – II./KG 2 had begun converting in October 1943 and would be followed by I./KG 2 at the end of March 1944.

Losses

Despite having 35 Do 217s, 20 Me 410s, 20 Fw 190s, 30 He 177s and 170 Ju 88/188s available for the first night of *Steinbock*, at least 16 Ju 88s, two Ju 188s, eight He 177s, one Fw 190, one Me 410 and four Do 217s were lost either to British defences or crashing to or from the target either due to technical problems or combat. In terms of the human cost, 74 aircrew were killed or missing, 15 captured and eight wounded or injured on the two raids this night. If such attacks were sustained and similar losses experienced, Peltz's ever-depleting bomber force would never be able to prosecute an effective campaign, something that Peltz realised very quickly.

Such losses were exacerbated by effective intruder operations, which successfully intercepted bombers on take-off or landing, or in transit from one airfield to another – the best example of this being the death of Maj Helmut Fuhrhop of I./KG 6 on 29 February 1944. Finally, German loss records for 1944 are incomplete as the records were lost, and unless a crew was

Crews from 604 Sqn briefing to counter the Luftwaffe. Sqn Dennis Furse is by the board, while far left his Nav/Rad Flt Lt Johnnie Downes looks on. This crew shot down their first aircraft, a Do 217 from 6./KG 2, on 28 April 1942 while flying with 406 Sqn. Both would go on to claim another three destroyed and four damaged, and would be awarded the DFC. (Author's collection)

killed, wounded or captured, one cannot be certain that other losses, such as when the crew baled out without a scratch, occurred; research for this book has revealed that such losses did occur back over the Continent, therefore further limiting available aircraft for future operations.

Targeting

General Dietrich Peltz never wanted to attack London or major cities, but that is what Hitler and Göring wanted. After the war, he best summed it up by saying:

> The attacks on London and other British cities were, in my opinion, like a few drops of water on a hot stone – a bit of commotion but after a very short time the whole thing was forgotten.

Then, when London was substituted by such targets as Hull and Bristol, poor navigation and pathfinding meant that most bombers, by now reduced in number by losses and unserviceability, failed to get anywhere near the stated target and even then, still suffered heavy losses.

Weather

General Dietrich Peltz realised that he had a problem in that he could not attack on moonlit nights because it made his crews even more vulnerable to RAF defences. Therefore, the initial commencement of the attack was scheduled for the end of December 1943's full moon period, which would have been around 31 December 1943/1 January 1944. This was then slipped until 21 January 1944, which was 11 days after the January full moon but the first night with acceptably reduced moonlight. However, he accepted quite early on:

> On moonless nights, the poor training of my crews meant that they were unlikely to find their targets.

Thus, bombing in moonless nights and at this time of the year in poor weather conditions, added to inaccurate pathfinding and limited bombing effectiveness. Poor weather forecasting also meant that flares dropped at altitude were quickly dispersed if the wind picked up. This was why the RAF pathfinder force used Mosquitoes to mark targets from low level with a higher degree of accuracy.

Conclusion

A series of factors meant that Operation *Steinbock* was generally seen as a failure and was a major factor in weakening the German bomber force in its efforts to counter the Allied invasion of Normandy on 6 June 1944. It can be best summed up by the following quote:

> It showed just how low the German bomber force's operational proficiency had sunk despite employing the full gamut of their electronic aids. It also showed how the technological superiority of the western Allies decided the outcome of *Steinbock*. Bravery, heroism, flying expertise, stubbornness, despair or suicide did not really help but at least it saved the lives of many British citizens.

The reason for the demise of so many German bombers during *Steinbock*: a Mosquito XIII, from 604 Sqn. (Author's collection)

ANALYSIS AND CONCLUSION

Unit	Type	Due to enemy action						Due to accidents					
		Jan	Feb	Mar	Apr	May	Total	Jan	Feb	Mar	Apr	May	Total
Stab/KG 2	Do 217 / Ju 188				1	1	2						0
I./KG 2	Do 217 / Ju 188	3	6	2	9	2	22	1	3	1	1	3	9
II./KG 2	Ju 188	1	7	4	9		21	2	2	1	1	1	7
III./KG 2	Do 217	6	5	11	13	4	39	3	1	3	3		10
V./KG 2	Me 410	7					7	1					1
Stab/KG 6	Ju 88 / Ju 188						0						0
I./KG 6	Ju 188	2	2	3		11	18	3	2	2		1	8
II./KG 6	Ju 88	3	8	5	5	2	23	5					5
III./KG 6	Ju 88	4	7	7	4		22	2			1		3
II./KG 30	Ju 88	7	2	9	5	5	28	3	1				4
I./KG 40	He 177	3			5	1	9	3	1	2		2	8
I./KG 51	Me 410			3	4		7		2	2	3	3	10
II./KG 51	Me 410		4		4	2	10				1	2	3
Stab/KG 54	Ju 88		1				1						0
I./KG 54	Ju 88	3	9	5	7	4	28	1		1	1		3
II./KG 54	Ju 88	3	4	6			13	7	1	1			9
I./KG 66	Ju 88 / Ju 188	5	9	5	11	1	31	2	2	2	1		7
Stab/KG 76	Ju 88						0						0
I./KG 76	Ju 88	4	1	1			6	1	1	1	1		4
I./KG 100	He 177	4	3	6	7	4	24	11	2	1	3	1	18
I./SKG 10	Fw 190	6	3	5	3	2	19		2		2	1	5
Total		61	70	73	87	39	330	45	20	17	18	14	114

These totals do not include those which suffered varying degrees of damage. Source: www.ww2.dk

Luftflotte 3 Orbat 13 June 1944			
Unit	Based	Aircraft	Commander
Stab/KG 2	Laon	Ju 188	Maj Franz Schönberger (stellv)
I./KG 2	Laon	Ju 188	Maj Franz Schönberger
II./KG 2	Laon	Ju 188	Maj Heinz Engel
III./KG 2	Laon	Do 217	Maj Albert Schreiweis
Stab/KG 6	Melsbroek	Ju 88	Obstlt Hermann Hogeback
I./KG 6	Brétigny	Ju 188	Hptm Wilhelm Traxlmayr (temporary)
II./KG 6	Villaroche	Ju 188	Maj Johann Mader
III./KG 6	Ahlhorn	Ju 188	Maj Rudolf Puchinger (+ 13 Jun 44)
Stab/KG 30	Zwischenahn	Ju 88	Obstlt Sigmund-Ulrich Frhr von Gravenreuth
II./KG 30	Zwischenahn	Ju 88	Maj Ernst Pflüger
II./KG 51	Soesterberg	Me 410	Hptm Karl-Egon Frhr von Dalwigk zu Lichtenfels
Stab/KG 54	Marx	Ju 88	Obstlt Riedesel Frhr von Eisenbach
I./KG 54	Wittmund	Ju 88	Hptm Ottfried Sehrt
III./KG 54	Marx	Ju 88	Maj Franz Zauner
I./KG 66	Avord	Ju 88S/Ju 188	Maj Hermann Schmidt
5./KG 76	Melsbroek	Ju 88	Maj Siegfried Geisler
Stab/LG 1	Le Culot	Ju 88	Obstlt Jochen Helbig
I./LG 1	Le Culot	Ju 88	Hptm Richard Czekay
II./LG 1	Chièvres	Ju 88	Maj Dieter Clemm von Hohenberg
I./SKG 10	Dreux	Fw 190	Maj Kurt Dahlmann

BIBLIOGRAPHY

Balke, Ulf, *Der Luftkrieg in Europa 1941–1945* (Bernard & Graefe Verlag, 1997)

Balke, Ulf, *Kampfgeschwader 100 'Wiking'* (Motorbuch Verlag, 1981)

Boiten, Theo, *Nachtjagd War Diaries Volume 2* (Wing Leader, 2011)

Bowyer, Michael, J. F., *Air Raid!* (Patrick Stephens Ltd, 1986)

Brütting, Georg, *Das waren die Deutschen Kampfflieger-Asse 1939–1945* (Motorbuch Verlag, 1977)

Foreman, John, *RAF Fighter Command Victory Claims of World War 3. Part 2 1943–1945* (Red Kite, 2012)

Goss, Chris, *Dornier Do 217: A Combat and Photographic Record* (Crecy, 2022)

Horn, Jan, *Das Flurschaden-Geschwader* (2010)

Kaiser, Jochen, *Der Ritterkreuzträger der Kampfflieger Band 1 & Band 2* (Luftfahrtverlag-Start, 2010)

Mackay, Ron, *The Last Blitz* (Red Kite, 2011)

Parker, Nigel, *Luftwaffe Crash Archive Volume 11* (Wing Leader, 2017)

Parry, Simon, *Intruders over Britain* (Air Research Publications, 1987)

Patzwall, Klaus, *Der Ehrenpokal für besondere Leistung im Luftkrieg* (Verlag Patzwall, 2008)

Price, Alfred, *Blitz on Britain 1939–45* (Ian Allan, 1977)

Scherzer, Veit, *Die Träger des Deutschen Kreuzes in Gold der Luftwaffe 1941–1945* (Scherzer Verlag, 1992)

Shores, Chris & Williams, Clive, *Aces High* (Grub Street, 1994)

Shores, Christopher, *Those Other Eagles* (Grub Street, 2004)

White, Ian, *The History of Air Interception Radar and the British Nightfighter 1935–1959* (Pen & Sword, 2007)

INDEX

Note: page numbers in bold refer to photographs, illustrations and captions.

AA (anti-aircraft) fire 21, **24**, 39, 45, **(47)**48–49, 50, 53, **55**, **69**, **78**, **87**
Abrahamczik, Oblt Rudolf 39, 40, **41**, 42
aircraft 31, 35, 74
   Avro Lancaster (UK) 53, 85
   Bristol Beaufighter (UK) 23, **42**, **45**, 64, **64**
   de Havilland Mosquito (UK) 21, 23, 25, 36, **42**, **45**, **45**, 64, 79, **79**, **80**, 80–81, 82, 85, **86**, 89, 91, **91**
   Dornier Do 17 (Germany) 9, **10**, **12**, 37, **70**, 79
   Dornier Do 217 (Germany) **5**, 7, 9, 10, **12**, 34, 40, **41**, 43, 44, **44**, **47**, 53, 58, 70, **70**, 74, 75, **(75)**76–**77**, 78, 79, **79**, 89, **90**
   Focke-Wulf Fw 190 (Germany) 6, 9, 11, 34, 39, 42, 43, 50, **60**, 61, 64, **64**, 67, 75, **75**, 78, **78**, 82, 85, 89
   Fw 190A-5 Jabo **16**
   Focke-Wulf Fw 200 (Germany) 35, 36, 71–74
   Hawker Typhoon (UK) 50, 57, **57 (71)**72–**73**
   Heinkel He 111 (Germany) 9, 10, **10**, 11–12, **34**, **41**, **63**, 82, 84
   Heinkel He 177 (Germany) 9, 11, **16**, 30, 31, **31**, 34, 35, **35**, 36, 38, 40, 41, 51, 53, 56, 59, 59–60, 74, 75, 78, 89
   Junker Ju 88 (Germany) 4, **6**, 9, 10, **12**, 13, **14**, 24, 30, **31**, 34, 37, 40, 45, 46, **(47)**48–**49**, 52, 53, 56, 58, **58**, 59, 60, 61, 64, **66**, 67, 70, **75**, 78, 79, 87, **88**, 89
   Ju 88S 6, **6**, 9, 10,**12**, 13, **14**, **56**, 59, 62, 75, 79
   Junkers Ju 188 (Germany) 6, **12**, **14**, 23, **36**, 40, 42, **45**, **46**, **47**, 53, **55**, 57, 62, **65**, **(71)**72–**73**, 75, 79, 80, 89
   Martin B-26 Marauder (US) 61, 64, 65
   Messerschmitt Me 262 (Germany) **41**, 85
   Messerschmitt Me 410 (Germany) 5, **6**, **8**, 9, 11, 13, 30, 34, 38, **38**, 39, **41**, 42, 43, 44, 50, 52, 53–56, 60–61, 64, 70, **71**, 74, 75, 79, 85, 89
   Supermarine Spitfire (UK) 64–65, 67

Baedeker Blitz, the 7, 28, 79
Barber, Phil 80
Barry, Fg Off John 56
Battle of Britain, the 7, 9, 10, **10**, 18, 28
Battle of France, the 7, 9, 28
Bein, Uffz Kurt 52
Bernsdorf, Uffz Eberhard 78
Billing, Ofw Alfred 37, 38
Bolten, Ofw Hermann 40, 42, 44, 50, 79, 85
bombing accuracy 32, **34**, 39, 53, 63, 67, **68**, 71, 79, 88, 91
bombing locations (map) **83**
bombloads 9, 10, 11, **12**, 30, 36, 38, 42, 43, 46, 51, 60, **83**
Botterbrodt, Oblt Helmut 35, 37, 39
Boyd, Wg Cdr Archibald 23
Braham, Wg Cdr Bob 59, **59**
Brandt, Uffz Heinz **88**
British Army, the
   1 AA Gp (1st Anti-Aircraft Gp) 21
   76th Heavy AA Rgt **24**
British assessments and reports 6, **(14)**15, 34, 43, 46, 50–51, 57, 67, **71**, 74–75, 79, 84
British defences (map) **(20)**21
British intelligence 6, 14, 39, 51, 52, **68**, **71**, 87
British strategy 18, 21, 44, 45, 46–47, **(47)**48–49, 57, 62, 65, **69**, 84, 89, 91
Britting, Oblt Karl-Reinhold **28**
Brochocki, Plt Off Jan 62
Budrat, Uffz Rudolf 51
Bunting, Sqn Ldr Nigel **61**, 64
Burbridge, Flt Lt Branse 52

chaff (Düppel) 14, 34, 36, 43, **55**, 82, 88
chronology of events 7
combat readiness 5–6, **6**
Condon, Fg Off Tom **66**
Crew, Wg Cdr Ed 70, **71**
crews 9, **12**, 13, 23, 36, 37, 38, 40, 42, 44, **85**, **88**
Cunningham, Wg Cdr John **24**, 25, 53

Dahlmann, Maj Kurt 89, 93
Davidson, Fg Off Paul 85
deaths 28, 29, **29**, 35, **35**, 38–39, 40, **40**, 41, 42, **42**, 43, **44**, 44–45, 46, 47, **47**, 50, 52, **52**, 53, 56, 57, **57**, **58**, 59, 60–61, 62, 64, 65, 66, 67, 70, 74, **75**, 75–78, 81, **81**, 82, 84, 85, 86, 89
Dessloch, Generaloberst Otto 28
Detal, Fg Off Charles **56**
diaries and memoirs 40, 42–43, **46**, 47–50, 52, 57, 59, 60, 63–64
Dieppe invasion, the 7
Dostlebe, Hptm Herbert 41, 71–74
Dovenmühle, Oblt Hans-Werner von der 35
Dowding system, the 18
Downes, Nav/Rad Flt Lt Johnnie **90**
Dyderski, Fw Helmut 66

Eastbourne railway station **60**
Eberspächer, Oblt Helmut 85
Edgar, Fg Off Johnnie 80, 81

Fara, Lt Ernst-Karl 67
fighter sweeps 57
Fisahn, Uffz Konrad 45, **45**
Fleischer, Ofw Hugo 35, 38–39
Fritz, Lt Wolfgang 47
Fuhrhop, Maj Helmut 29, **42**, **46**, 47, **56**, 56–57, **57**, 89
Furse, Sqn Ldr Dennis **90**

GCI 'Happidromes' 18, **22(23)**
German airfields (map) **(26)**27
German strategy and tactics 4, 8, 14, 16–17, 26, 28, 30–34, 35, 38, 39–44, 45–50, 51–56, 55, 60–67, **68–69**, 70–79, **71**, 81–85, **85**, 86–88, 89, 90–91
Goebbels, Dr Joseph 4
Göring, Reichsmarschall Hermann 4, **4**, 5, 7, 8, 26, 28, 30, 90
GORs (Gun Operations Rooms) 21

Hailbronner, Oblt Rolf 56–57
Haine, Wg Cdr Dick **61**
Hall, Flt Lt John **61**, 64
Hallensleben, Obstlt Rudolf 29, **29**
Hampshire, Wg Cdr Keith 25, **66**
Hanke, Ofw Georg 29
Haschle, Oblt Rudolf **36**
Hein, Oblt Alfred 70, **70**
Heinrich, Fw Otto 29, **81**, 82
Heintz, Hptm Kurt 29, **38**, 39
Heisig, Hptm Helmut **63**, 64
Henderson, Air Vice-Marshal Malcolm 18
Heney, Sqn Ldr Harold 85
Hibbert, Fg Off Stan 40
Hill, Air Marshal Sir Roderic 18, **61**
Hitler, Adolf 8, 28, 40
Hogeback, Oberst Hermann **28**, 29, **58**, 86, **93**
Holle Generalleutnant Alexander 28
Holst, Uffz Ernst 47, 52

IAZ (London Inner Artillery Zone), the 21
Imperial German Army, the 26
intruder missions **8**, 9, 11, 44, 45, 46, 51, 56–57, **57**, 60, 65, 70, 71, 74, 78, 79, 84, 85, 89

Kalckreuth, Hptm Hans-Gotthelf von 51
Kelsey, Nav/Rad WO Georg **82**, 84

Kemp, WO Howard **35**, 36
Kennedy, Flt Lt Ken 67
Kessel, Obstlt Karl 29
Kesselring, Generalfeldmarschall Albert 28
Kettenhund jammers 79, 88
kill claims 39, 40, 45, 47, 50, 51, **51**, 52, 53, 56, 57, 59, 62, 63, 64, 70, **75**, 78, 82, 84, 85, 90
Kneath, Fg Off Barry **82**, 84
Knode, Uffz Heinz 65
Korten, Generaloberst Günther 40
Krahner, Lt Wolfgang 64, **64**

Lahl, Lt Günther 52, 53
Laubman, Fg Off Don 64–65
Leigh-Mallory, Sir Trafford 18
Lelong, Fg Off Roy 85
Lenkheit, Lt Hans-Friedrich 42, 47, 52, 65
Lissat, Hptm Erwin 65, 82
Lohf, Fw Wilhelm 50, 85
Luftwaffe, the 7, 14, 63, 70, 86, **87**
   8th Abteilung 35
   IX Fliegerkorps 4–5, **6**, 11, 29, 30
   Kampfgeschwader (KG) 4–5
     KG 2 **6**, 7, 9, **12**, 29, **69**, 79, 82, **84**, 85, 89, **92**, **93**
     I./KG 2 45, 53, 58, 89
     II./KG 2 89
     III./KG 2 **5**, 45, 58
     Stab I./KG 2 39, 53, 79, **92**
     V./KG 2 **6**, **8**, 11, 29, **38**, 39, 42, 43, 44, 50, 52
     KG 6 **5**, **6**, **28**, 29, 45, **69**, 82, 86, **92**, **93**
     I./KG 6 29, **29**, **42**, **46**, **56**, 56–57, **57**, **58**, 61, 79, 86, 89
     II./KG 6 29, 30, **55**, 62, 86, 87
     III./KG 6 **28**, 29, 40, 58, 86
     KG 26
     III./KG 26 11, 16, **41**
     KG 27 82
     KG 30 30, 60, **69**, **92**, **93**
     II./KG 30 75, 79
     III./KG 30 75
     KG 40 **16**, **92**
     I./KG 40 9, 31, 35, 36, 38, 39, 41, 78
     II./KG 40 7, 39, 40–41, 78
     KG 51 **44**, 82, 89, **92**, **93**
     I./KG 51 **5**, **8**, 11, 30, 60, 61, 71, 79, 84–85
     II./KG 51 (V./KG 2) **8**, 11, 13, 39, 40, 52, 56, 70, 74, 79, 84, 85
     III./KG 51 **56**, 82
     Stab II./KG 51 74, 78
     KG 53
     Stab II./KG 53 **10**
     KG 54 29, 30, 50, 89, **92**, **93**
     I./KG 54 **(47)**48–**49**, **55**, 70, 79
     II./KG 54 16, **55**
     Stab/KG 54 **47**
     KG 60
     I./KG 60 (II./KG 77) 29
     KG 66 **6**, **92**, **93**
     Einsatzstaffel I./KG 66 59
     I./KG 66 6, 10, 12, 13, 14, **14**, 29, 45, **(47)**48–**49**, **55**, **56**, 59, **62**, 65, **65**, **69**, **75**, 79
     KG 76 29, **29**, 30, **92**, **93**
     I./KG 76 58
     II./KG 76 29
     KG 77
     II./KG 77 28–29
     Stab./KG 77 28
     KG 100 **16**, **92**
     I./KG 100 9, 30, 31, 35, 38, **(47)**48–**49**, 61, 78, 89
     III./KG 100 74 **(75)**76–**77**, 78

INDEX

KG 101
    Einsatzstaffel Verbandsführerschule **44**, 45, **45**, 50, 52, 70, 75, 79
Kampfgruppen (KGrzbV)
    KGrzbV 100 11, 16, 65
Legion Condor 26, 40, 56, **56**, 70, **70**
Luftflotte 2 16, 28, 30
Luftflotte 3 5, 7, 16, 26, 28, 30, 79, 81, 88, **93**
Schnellkampfgeschwader (SKG)
    SKG 10
    I./SKG 10 6, **6**, 11, **16**, 39, 40, 42, 43, 50, **60**, 61, **63**, 64, **64**, 67, 70, 79, **81**, 85, 89, **92**, **93**
staffeln
1./KG 6 42, **79**, 79–80
1./KG 40 31, 35, 36, 37, 38, 40, 41, 89
1./KG 51 70, 71, **71**
1./KG 54 63
1./KG 55 40
1./KG 100 42
2./KG 2 53
2./KG 6 **36**, **40**, 42, 65, 82
2./KG 40 31, 35, 37, 38, 40, 89
2./KG 51 **41**, **56**
2./KG 54 59
2./KG 66 34, 52, 62, **67**, **(71)72–73**
2./KG 76 **10**, **29**
2./KG 100 **16**, **31**, 36, 41, 51, 59, **59**, 62, 71–74, 75–78, 89
2./KGrzbV 1 36
2./SKG 10 6, 42, 50
3./KG 2 **44**, 44, 53, 79
3./KG 4 38
3./KG 40 35
3./KG 54 24, 46, **88**, 89
3./KG 100 29, 31, 35, 41, 51, 56, 59, 60, 89
3./SKG 10 29, 42, **75**, 78, **78**, 82
3./SKG 120 85
4./KG 2 **56**, 70
4./KG 4 50, 59
4./KG 6 **43**, 47, 53, 59, 65–66, 67, 78, 87
4./KG 30 61, **61**, 64
4./KG 51 **74**, 79, 85
4./KG 54 87
5./KG 2 70, **70**, 79
5./KG 6 40, 62, **75**, 78, 84
5./KG 30 63
5./KG 51 29, 74, 85
6./KG 2 **90**
6./KG 3 70
6./KG 6 29, **29**, **52**, 57, **66**
6./KG 30 63
6./KG 52 74, 85
6./KG 77 28
8./KG 6 (8./LG 1) **28**, 61, 64
8./KG 51 39
9./KG 6 40
9./KG 54 **75**, 78
9./KG 55 **29**
9./KG 76 **31**
9./KG 100 **75**, 78
9./LG 1 39
11./KG 2 79
13./KG 2 **8**
14./KG 2 39, 40, **41**, 42, 44, 46, 52
16./KG 2 **52**
Stukasgeschwader (StG) 28

Mader, Maj Johann 29, 86, 87, **93**
Maidment, Flt Sgt Jim **35**, 36
Maier, Hptm Kurt 29, 35
Manowarda, Oblt Karl von 42, **79**, 79–80
matèriel losses 6, 7, 9, 23, 34–35, 39, 40, 41, 43, 45, 46, **47**, 50, 51–52, 53–55, 56, **56**, 59, 60–61, 62, 64, 70, 71, 74, 75, **(75)**76–77, 81, 82, 89–**90**, **90**, 92–**93**
medals and honours 4, 26, 28, **28**, 29, **29**, **32**, 35–36, **38**, 38–39, 40, **41**, **51**, **56**, 56–57, 59, 62, **62**, 64, 65, 70, **70**, 74, 75, **81**, 82, 84, **84**, 87, **90**
Melcher, Lt Rolf-Heinrich 35, 38
military strength and complements 6, **6**, 9, **17**, 23, 89
Miller, Wg Cdr Charles 70

Mirbach, Ofw Erwin 36
Möller, Lt Herbert 78, **78**
Moore, Plt Off Gregor 78
Moulin, Fg Off Charles De 57
Müller, Fw Karl 52
Müller, Hptm Heinrich 62
Müller, Lt Felix 52
Müller, Oblt Hugo 38, 41

navigation and bombing systems **(26)27**, 88–89
    Freya EGON 12, **13**, 32–34, 40
    Hyperbel Gerät 12, 34
    Knickebein 11, 12, **34**, 63, **75**
    OBOE 12
    X-Verfahren and X-Gerät 11, 16, **34**
    Y-Verfahren and Y-Gerät 11–12, 16, **27**, 32–34, 40, **41**
Needham, Flt Lt Barry 64–65, **65**
night missions 5, 7, 9, 16, **16**, **(75)**76–77, 81, 90–91
nightfighters 5, 9, 11, 21, **23**, 23–24, 34, 47, 60, 64, 70, 79, **79**, 84, 89

obsolescence 9, **10**, 89
Oeben, Hptm Anton **66**
orders of battle **17**, **25**, 89

Pahl, Oblt Richard 70, **71**
Palme, Lt Herbert **75**, 78
Pape, Oblt Werner 60
Parge, Fw Günther **43**, 47, 50, 53, 59, 65–66, 67, 87
Pargeter, Flt Lt Reg **51**, 56
Parker-Rees, Sqn Ldr Alastair 6, 39
Parpart, Lt Roderich von 53
pathfinding and target marking 6, **8**, 9, 10, 11, 13–14, **14**, **(14)15**, 35, 38, 39, **41**, 42, 43, 45, **47**, 50, **55**, 61, 63, **69**, 79, 81, 82, 88, 90, 91
Peltz, Generalmajor Dietrich 4, 5, **5**, 8, 9, 11, 26, **26**, **28**, 28–29, 31–32, 40, 47, 50, **62**, 89, 90
Petrasch, Lt Walter **52**
Pfeffer, Hptm Herbert **75**, 78
pilot experience 5, 9, 11, 23, **29**, 38, 39, 40, 51, 60, 63, **63**, 64, 65, 71, **71**, 75, 79, 85, 87, 88
Plate, Oblt Helmut 50
POWs 51, 53, 67, **68**
predictor 24
production 9, **10**, 19
Provan, Fg Off Bill 56
Puchinger, Maj Rudolf **28**, 29, **58**, 86, **93**
Puttfarken, Hptm Dietrich 29, 74

radar systems 9, 14, 79, 88
    AI (Airborne Interception) radar 9, **23**, 23–25, 89
    AMES GCI (Ground-Controlled Interceptor) Types 18–21, **19**, **22(23)**, 34, 89
RAF, the 5, 6, 8, 9, 14, 16, 32, 36, 50–51, 59, 62, 79, 89
    13 OTU **51**
    42 OTU 74
    80 Wing **69**
    Fighter Command 18
        ADBG (Air Defence of Great Britain) 18, **20**, 21, **22**, 23, **25**, 61, **69**
    fighter groups 18
    squadrons
        25 Sqn 51, 62, 85
        29 Sqn **42**, 56
        50 Sqn 85
        68 Sqn 23, 40, **75**, 78, 82
        85 Sqn 24, 25, 37, 39, 52, 53, **63**, **70**, 75
        96 Sqn 6, 39, 40, 50, 52, 59, 64, 67, 70, **86**
        97 Sqn 84
        105 Sqn 85
        125 Sqn 23, 82
        151 Sqn **35**, 36, **82**
        174 Sqn 50
        219 Sqn 23
        263 Sqn 44, **44**
        264 Sqn 74, **79**, **80**
        266 Sqn **(71)72–73**
        307 Sqn 62
        331 Sqn 56
        379 Sqn 56
        406 Sqn 23, **75**, 78
        409 Sqn 23, **45**, **64**

        410 Sqn 40, 45, 64
        412 Sqn 64–65, **65**
        418 Sqn 46
        456 Sqn 23, **66**, 71, 82
        488 Sqn **61**, 64
        582 Sqn 85
        604 Sqn 23, **45**, 64, 82, **90**, **91**
        605 Sqn 45, 85
        609 Sqn **56**, 57, **57**
        613 Sqn **59**
        619 Sqn 95
raids 33
    April 1944 **70**, 70–75, **(71)72–73**
        Plymouth (30 April) **(75)**76–77, 78, **78**
    February 1944 42–56, **54–55**
    January 1944 32–42, **38**
    March 1944 59, 60–63, 64–67, **65**, **67**
        Bristol (27–28 March) 67, **68–69**
    May 1944 79–84, 88
        Portsmouth (22 May) 82, **84**
Ramsey, Flt Lt Charles **79**, 80–81
ranges 9, 10, 11, 23, 24, 37, 80
Rath, Maj Wilhelm 82, **84**
Reed, Flt Lt C. P. **61**, 64
Riedesel Freiherr zu Eisenbach, Obstlt Volprecht 29
Robinson, Nav/Rad Fg Off G. D. **45**
Rommel, Generalfeldmarschall Erwin 42
routes and targets (map) **(32)33**
Runge, Stfw Otto 39
Ruppe, Ofw Wolfgang 51

Sanders, Flt Lt Arthur 71
Saunders, Air Vice-Marshal Hugh 18
Schiml, Ogefr Erich **40**, 42–43, 45, 46, **46**, 47–50, 52, 53, 56, 59, 60, 61, 63–64
Schmidt, Maj Hermann 13, 29, **62**, 65, **65**, **93**
Schmitt, Hptm Walter 34, 62
Schüttke, Hptm Helmut 40
Schwartz, Uffz Erich 84
Schwegler, Hptm Mathias 'Teddy' **44**, 45
searchlights **27**, 36, 42–43, 47, 50, 53, 60, 63, 65–66, **69**, **75**, 79, 80, 81, **87**
service ceilings 10, 11, 23
Seyfarth, Hptm Kurt **32**
Singleton, Flt Lt Joe 62
Somerville, Sqn Ldr Dean 45, **45**
speeds 10, 11, **12**, 23, 64
Sperrle, Generalfeldmarschall Hugo 5, 7, 26, **26**, 28
Steele, Air Vice-Marshal Charles 18
Störangriff sorties 30, 43, 50, 61, 64, 67, 70, 71, 79

technical issues 11, 38, 65
Thurner, Hptm Johann 29, **29**, 57, 58, 86
Thwaites, Sqn Ldr Bernard **63**, 64
training 23, 28, 45, 56, 74, 82, 87
Trialen and bomb damage 87

USAAF, the 8, 28, 61, 64, 74

Vincent, Air Vice-Marshal Stanley 18

Wachtler, Uffz Franz 44, 46
Warnes, Sqn Ldr Geoff **44**, **44**
Waterbeck, Ofw Karl 35–36, 39
weaponry 23, **37**, 42, 53
    3.7in AA gun (UK) **19**, 21, **21**, **(47)48–49**
    1000kg bomb (Germany) **29**, 38, 51, 80,**83**
    2000kg HE bomb (Germany) 36
    AB1000 bomb (Germany) 42, 43, 53, **58**, 60
    Fritz X guided bomb (Germany) 8, **74**, **75**
    SB1000 bomb (Germany) 44, 46
    SC2000 bomb (Germany) 36, **37**
    UP-3 rocket (UK) **(47)48–49**
    Z battery (UK) **18**, 21, **(47)48–49**
weather conditions 13, **27**, 31, **33**, 34, 35, 39, 40, 42, 51, 61, **71**, 81, 89, 91
Wells, Sqn Ldr Johnnie 57
Wenning, Lt Wolfgang 74, 78
Werner, Elfriede 59
Werner, Lt Wilhelm **59**, 59–60
Williams, Fg Off Ernest 52, 53
Wolf, Lt Eginhart 61, **61**, 64
Wood, Flt Sgt J. L. **6**